THE CONSTRAINTS OF
CORPORATE TRADITION

THE CONSTRAINTS
OF CORPORATE
TRADITION

*DOING THE CORRECT THING, NOT
JUST WHAT THE PAST DICTATES*

ALAN M. KANTROW

1817

HARPER & ROW, PUBLISHERS, New York

*Cambridge, Philadelphia, San Francisco, Washington
London, Mexico City, São Paulo, Singapore, Sydney*

FIRST EDITION

Designer: *Sidney Feinberg*
Copyeditor: *Ann Finlayson*
Indexer: *Sydney Cohen*

Library of Congress Cataloging-in-Publication Data
Kantrow, Alan M., 1947
  The constraints of corporate tradition.
  Includes index.
  1. Corporate culture. 2. Organizational
effectiveness. 3. Industrial management. I. Title.
HD58.7.K375 1987   302.3'5   86–46075
ISBN 0–06–015753–4

87 88 89 90 91 HC 10 9 8 7 6 5 4 3 2 1

For Dave Dyer, George Smith, Meg Graham,
and David Allen—friends and colleagues who know better
than anyone else that the past is not just prologue.

Contents

Preface

When asked by a peremptory hostess what he thought of a certain unmemorable dessert, Winston Churchill is said to have replied, "Madam, it is a pudding without a theme." For the better part of the past decade, by virtue of my association with *Harvard Business Review*, and more recently with the Winthrop Group, a consulting firm specializing in business history, I have been seated at the ever-expanding banquet of research and writing on management. Most of it has been delightful and instructive. But now I push my chair back from the table with much the same reaction as Sir Winston. The medley of insights, valuable results, and important findings lingers upon the tongue. But something is missing and has been missing all along. With few exceptions, the great helpings of prose and urgent advice under which managers increasingly find themselves buried reads as if the past—of an individual, a company, a product, an issue—were thoroughly irrelevant to present concerns or, at best, an ornamental reminder of other days and other times. The banquet has lacked a theme, and the theme is history—institutional memory.

Organizations remember—sometimes accurately, frequently not, sometimes with an awareness that that is what they are doing, most often in happy oblivion that their past has any ongoing call on their time or attention. Yet institutions do remember all the time. The style of a business presentation, the kinds of evidence that tend to sway decisions, the shared sense of what constitutes relevant information about a new market or product, the deep-seated visceral preference for certain lines of business—all these characteristics, and a thousand others like them, are the subtle products of memory. In no two organizations are they exactly the same, nor in any two parts of the same organization. Our individual experience of history is, after all, just that: individual.

Intuitively, we know this. But on the job we usually disregard it. Recently, however, the frustration of a tougher competitive environment and the limitations of purely quantitative management techniques have rekindled explicit interest in the softer side of how people think, decide, and act in corporate settings. In a way, this fall from economic grace has offered a salutary reminder that being a competent manager does not mean checking at the door of our office our general understanding of how people think in groups. Now more than ever, it means quite the opposite. We need to be able to call upon the full range of who we are, what we know, and what—and how—we remember.

If we cannot—or worse, we will not—then we must

settle for the inadequacies of more limited efforts to make sense of the softer side of things. Today's popular infatuation with the notion of corporate culture, for example, will quickly fade into disenchantment if we do not give over the simpleminded effort to manipulate it as if it were a dial that can be spun or reset at will—that is, if we do not stop trying, for example, to turn an old-line manufacturing firm overnight into an organization that behaves like a high-tech start-up. Otherwise, lacking a sense of history and an appreciation of how organizations remember, we are sorely tempted to view culture as the convenient label of choice for all sorts of villainless failures. When bright ideas miscarry, when clever strategies disappear in the execution, when well-wrought plans sink without a trace, faddish notions of culture provide a ready and blameless explanation.

Is a product late? Culture held it up. Is market expansion behind schedule? Culture got in the way. Is a plant slow to adopt new technology? Culture is the mother of resistance. Is a new division head unable to command the loyalty of the division's old hands? Culture is the mother of intransigence. Is it hard to get full discussion of unpleasant facts? Culture is the enemy of truth. Is effective follow-up an infrequent visitor in executive ranks? Culture holds the door shut against it. Nary a corporate sparrow falls without disappearing into the La Brea tar pit of culture.

The point is not that cultural explanations are useless. Far from it. We desperately need the insights they can provide. But what possible sense are we to make of the label mongering that so often masquerades under the banner of cultural analysis? What possible basis for action does it provide? What in the world does it mean to say that culture breeds intransigence? It may be true in a given situation, but what does it mean? And how can we use our knowledge of its meaning? These labels will inevitably prove blank and barren—unless we push behind them to an understanding of the deeper mechanisms that create the patterns we so much wish to comprehend. That is, unless we give up our reliance on easy labels and look, instead, to the hidden processes by which institutions actually remember, the processes by which they take possession of their history.

There are certain kinds of knowledge from which there is no turning back. They change forever the way we see the world. In Act II of *The Winter's Tale*, Shakespeare puts a telling image of such knowing into the mouth of a jealous king. Should a venomous spider fall, by chance, into the cup of wine, "one may drink, depart/ And yet partake no venom; for his knowledge/ Is not infected. . . ." But should that spider once be seen, the venom will inexorably do its work. The king, alas, believes he has indeed "drunk, and seen the spider." Perhaps he has. Once we have grown aware of the many ways in which the force of history makes itself felt in the present, *we* surely have. *We* cannot go back. Certainly, I cannot, for I was trained first as an anthropologist and then as a historian.

This book is an effort to pay for my dinner. Cup in hand, I have something I very much want to say about

the force of history, of memory, in corporate affairs—
about its implications for the tasks and responsibilities of
management. And I want to say it not as a set piece from
behind a rostrum, but informally, dinner guest to dinner
guest. So, amid the clamor at our end of the table, please
lend an ear for a moment or two. There is some conversation, good old-fashioned talk, that we can profitably
have together.

This talk is very much intended to be a reminder of
things already familiar but all too prone to slip out of
mind. Like it or not, the past infects the world we live
in, the decisions we make, the very choices we see to lie
before us. If we ignore its influence, we do not escape its
power. All we do is remain to some extent its prisoners
without ever really knowing that that is what we are. If,
however, we acknowledge it, learn to recognize its workings, come to greet it on familiar terms, we can put it to
excellent use.

This is not an abstract plea for the disembodied value
of the liberal arts. Not at all. It is an argument, a strong
pitch after a good meal, for the practical value of looking
along with me into the cup. We can find there something
eminently worth having. Nor is this a disguised plea for
setting up yet another category of corporate expert to
whom we can delegate matters historical—while, of
course, finding gainful employment for legions of un- or
underemployed historians. It is a reminder, dinner guest
to dinner guest, that these are things we had better
worry about ourselves.

These things are not idle matters with no real bearing

on corporate performance. A maker of computer periph-
erals like disk drives or color monitors comes to grief
because its people are so used to viewing the world in a
certain way that they cannot see how much their market
has become a systems market. . . . A financial institution
persists in ignoring the threat posed by the in-house
financial operations of capital goods producers like GE or
GM. . . . A capital budgeting scheme designed to move
a commodity producer of metals downstream toward
manufactured end products fails to skew the pattern of
investment. . . . Domestic manufacturers pump massive
infusions of capital into new flexible technologies like
robotics but continue to use them in high-volume, low-
variety environments. . . . In all these cases history is
making itself felt. Of course, in each of these instances
there are other forces at work. But we are, for the most
part, able to recognize them with some ease. It is the
unseen, subterranean influence of history—institutional
memory—that regularly eludes us.

How to go about the task of capturing it?

First, we owe it to ourselves to recognize that our
day-to-day views of things—our assumptions, certainties, the very categories we use to structure our experience—are not just "there" in the nature of things, hard
facts to be taken up at need. They are, instead, the
cumulative product of artifice, selection, and manipulation. They are "built" or constructed in the same way
that a work of art is. In practice, however, we forget the
artifice that shapes them and treat them as if they were
hard nuggets of fact.

Chapter I is my dinner-table way of saying, Hey, wait a minute. Let's not forget the artifice. Let's not forget that the world in which we operate is a "built" environment. It did not have to turn out the way it did. Other outcomes, other mixtures and combinations, were possible. What lies before us, then, is the unique result of a unique series of events, a unique set of overlays that have been built up over time the way a coral reef is. To see historically, we first have to see *through* the orderly assumptions and conventions we accept so matter-of-factly to the chaotic experiences out of which they have slowly been precipitated. We have to be able to see, for example, that the unexpectedly sticky substance turned up by a laboratory experiment is not a failed structural material—as the nature of our search has led us to expect—but a powerful new kind of adhesive.

Chapter II then poses a simple question. If we move in a "built" environment, where did the pieces come from with which we have done the building? They did not simply happen to be there but were made available to us through the highly selective operation of tradition, the institutional mechanism for passing along relevant shreds and patches from past experience. Tradition, though, is a funny creature. Not only does it serve as a conduit for such odds and ends. It also makes them available to us in ways that elicit our interest and, more than that, our commitment and our loyalty. It energizes us, but in the process it binds us unthinkingly to established modes of doing things and established categories of thought. It also enables us to forget what it leaves out.

We had, therefore, better understand something about the hold that tradition has on us, especially since we so easily fail to notice that it has any hold on us at all. Otherwise, we risk forgetting—as GM has done in backing away from the initial boldness of its Saturn experiment or from its involvement of an outsider like H. Ross Perot in the deliberations of its board—that our past holds a richer universe of experience than current self-definition acknowledges.

But there is more. What we know through tradition does not sit neatly in this or that corner of our experience. It is a contagious form of knowledge and infects almost everything with which it comes into contact. Accordingly, Chapter III is an effort to bring the mechanics of contagion—our tendency to reason by a kind of slippery and inexact analogy—into focus, much as medical researchers work to identify just how some particular virus does its work. Once we understand these mechanics, we have a greatly improved chance of intervening in the process without giving up what is of value to us in the operation of tradition.

Finally, Chapter IV wonders aloud how our careful interventions can do more than just help protect us against such contagion. Freed to explore *all* the past in which we have a stake, not just those portions that tradition has silently passed along to us, we are much better able to make of our past a usable, and not an imprisoning, resource. AT&T, after all, is not just a long regulated behemoth trying to learn what competition is all about. It is also a company that, in its early years, was as scrappy and as bare-knuckles competitive as any other new start-up.

These may seem, at first glance, odd concerns to press upon managers. My sincere hope is that the talk that follows—at least at our end of the table—will make their value clear.

THE CONSTRAINTS OF
CORPORATE TRADITION

I

A Hardening of the Categories

The difficulty is, e'en on the face of 'em the facts are dark—doubly so if you grant, as wise men must, that an ill deed can be done with good intent, and a good with ill; and triply if you hold right and wrong to be like windward and leeward, that vary with standpoint, latitude, circumstance, and time. History, in short, is like those waterholes I have heard of in the wilds of Africa: the most various beasts may drink there side by side with equal nourishment.

—JOHN BARTH, *The Sot-Weed Factor*

EVEN THE MOST BULLISH denizen of Wall Street does not look upon the World Trade Center and think that, only a week ago, the site was open ground, filled with the garden plots of early Dutch settlers. Even the most enthusiastic snapper of photos at the rim of the Grand Canyon does not imagine that, barely a month before, this was a level expanse. Even the most ardent Sinophile does not believe the Great Wall was the creation of a moment. Day to day, we all understand that some things take time, that what we see before us is the cumulative result of long and often complex activity. We all know, without having to be told, that the world around us is a world gradually built up by human effort and natural process. But when we go to work, we forget.

In particular, we forget both the density and duration of the activity underlying the surface facts with which we deal. We forget that, like an iceberg, nine tenths of their mass lies hidden, well below the normal waterline of vision. And we forget that the part we can see is not just "there" but is very much something built, something constructed or pieced together over time.

Corporations, the institutions of modern commerce, are such constructed things, and the work that managers do takes place in such "built" environments. Phrased so baldly, the point seems obvious. But in the normal course of events—and, especially, in terms of how we regularly talk and think about the work of management—the point disappears from view. As a practical matter, we do not commonly treat a corporation as the cumulative result of an historical process of development, nor do we think of it in the present as an edifice held together by the bricks and mortar of tradition. Yet it is, and we should.

Why bother? What possible difference does it make? Is there any conceivable benefit from thinking this way? Is there any serious danger to which our usual forgetfulness at work exposes us? The chapters that follow attempt to answer these questions in a way that makes sense to managers as well as to other thoughtful observers of modern institutional life. More to the point, these later chapters try to make sense out of what it actually means to carry out the work of management in contexts that are, whether we like it or not, rich with tradition, things inherited and passed on.

Here, though, in Chapter I we start with a simpler task: establishing the grounds for looking at the modern corporation as a thing constructed out of such bits and pieces. But to do that, we must first have a general look at the way the world around us gets built every day by the imposition of categories on a jumbled mass of experience. That is, we must look hard at the raw fact of artifice in arrangements that usually strike us as perfectly natural. If we don't, we cannot hope to tell which parts of those arrangements truly lie beyond our control and which we can, if we will, influence. No one can alter the sunrise; but what men have made, men can change— and manage.

Examining this raw fact of artifice is where we begin: The opening sections of this chapter look from a variety of angles at the many constructs and conventions that make the world we move in so much of a "built" environment. From that world, however, our awareness of artifice rapidly disappears. In a word, we quickly forget that what lies about us is not so much given in the nature of things but is, rather, the cumulative product of human effort over time. Is there anything that can restore lost awareness? Yes, indeed: the recovery through institutional memory, through history, of salient facts about the many pieces of things that make up our constructed world. Effective memory helps us see artifice for what it is. Does such clear vision matter—especially, does it

matter to managers? Absolutely. Showing that it does—
and showing why—is the work of this chapter.

Dividing up the World

In the late summer of 1914, or so Walter Lippmann tells
the story, a small group of Englishmen, Frenchmen, and
Germans lived together on an island that had no contact
with the outside world except through a British mail
steamer that arrived once every two months. Waiting
eagerly to hear the outcome of a particularly juicy murder trial, these friends learned instead that their countries had been at war for nearly six weeks. Here they had
been acting on fairly intimate terms when in fact they
were, in a technical sense at least, the most bitter of
enemies.

An officer on the staff of General Joffre, the hero of
the Marne, reports that a photographer who came to do
a portrait of this lionized savior of France could not proceed until aides tacked up a series of maps on the walls.
After all, popular imagination demanded that so great a
general's office be covered with maps. A barren
worktable in a spare, mapless, middle-class office simply
would not do.

In such circumstances as these, we can fairly quickly
see that the categories of social reality through which we
move are not "there" in the same way that rocks or
earthquakes are. Dr. Johnson, the great eighteenth-
century English man of letters, could disprove the old
philosophical argument that things do not exist in them-

selves by giving a nearby stone a sharp kick. A bruised toe and a tumbling bit of quartz are pretty convincing evidence for the existence of rocks. But how do we prove with equal certainty who *our* friends are? Would *we* believe in the image of a military hero behind a bureaucrat's desk?

In one form or other, these questions come up all the time. Data do not become information until we are able to see the patterns in them, to see which bits and pieces cluster together in some kind of order. And the existence of some mode of order, in turn, deeply influences how we regard the next snippet of data that comes along. If our island neighbors are friends, we know how to treat them and how to interpret their actions. But when the mail steamer arrives, things again become complicated, and we have to juggle old packages of facts into new categories. This juggling may be awkward or painful, but we cannot do without it.

Our social environment is so immense, so complex, so riddled with opinion and belief, so rapidly changing, so much a construct of our own assumptions and expectations, and often so unknowable that we cannot—even if we wanted to—deal with it directly. We can kick a stone to rearrange a landscape, but we cannot so readily tell friend from foe. To act in so problematic an environment, to travel with purpose in such a world, we must first keep maps of that world in our heads. The problem, as Lippmann counsels, is to "secure maps on which [our] own need, or someone else's need, has not sketched in the coast of Bohemia."

Repair work on our categories for things is what mapmaking is all about. Indeed, drawing or borrowing or revising such maps is something we do all the time. We act "not on direct knowledge, but on pictures" that we create or that others create for us. Our categories matter. They have grave consequences for how we act and why.

> If [a man's] atlas tells him that the world is flat he will not sail near what he believes to be the edge of our planet for fear of falling off. If his maps include a fountain of eternal youth, a Ponce de Leon will go in quest of it. If someone digs up yellow dirt that looks like gold, he will for a time act exactly as if he has found gold. The way in which the world is imagined determines at any particular moment what men will do. It does not determine what they will achieve. It determines their effort, their feelings, their hopes, not their accomplishments and results.[1]

In the modern corporation, no explosion of personal computers, no new telecommunications gear or software packages, no eight-color strategic matrix or refinement of ROI calculations—in short, none of the technical apparatus of management—can change this situation one whit. The woman at her desk in a corner office, no matter how sophisticated the equipment at her elbow, does not deal with the world directly but only through the maps of it—the categories—she carries in her head. More accurately, she deals with it through the refinements that she has been provided by others, whose job it is to distill such charts and plottings for her out of the infinite mass of available data. Even in the best of circumstances, she can know the world only at several removes.

To repeat: categories matter. There is neither world enough nor time to deal with every new bit of data as if we had never seen anything remotely like it before. We simply must have ways to group things, labels to give them—even if those labels have distorting side effects we would rather do without. Here, for instance, is James L. Ferguson, the CEO of General Foods, talking about the way in which his company—like many others—thinks about individual businesses:

> Coffee is a good case in point. Naturally, our coffee business had been classified as a cash cow, or maintenance product. In point of fact, however, this is a very volatile and dynamic business. For example, in recent years, with the advent of automatic coffee makers in the home, there has been a lot of activity in the ground-coffee market to develop new varieties of ground coffees. We didn't miss these opportunities, but I believe we were a little late and not as aggressive in pursuing them because of the cash-cow concept.[2]

A manager would have had to spend the past dozen years in a Tibetan monastery not to recognize here the apparatus of modern strategic planning. For the large modern corporation with a range of businesses under its control, there must be some responsible way to determine the claim each has on available resources. There must be some agreed-on language for saying, Now this is how we think about the prospects and the requirements of the coffee business. In short, there must be categories, and a principle of categorization. The problem, of course, is that the facts are usually more complicated and qualified than such principles admit and that simplifying them by affixing a label is often a form of self-fulfilling prophecy. If a map says the world is flat, no sailor— certainly none that works on salary plus bonus—will venture too near the edge. Without a map, however, few would ever leave port. Approximate knowledge may be faulty. It may even bias action in an unintended direction. But we cannot do without it. We must have something to go on, some basis for starting out toward this instead of that point on the horizon. We must have categories, however imperfect, to work with and from. If we waited for perfect knowledge, we would stay forever in port. More to the point, we would never even build a ship.

Philosophical objections that our knowledge cannot draw us a true map of the world are, in this sense, irrelevant. We do not have the luxury of refusing to sail. After all, there has to be some basis for allocating resources to the coffee business. Die-hard philosophers may wring their hands and object, but a swift Johnsonian kick in the rear ought to quiet all doubts. In practice, managers do know enough to act. Case closed.

Well, not quite. However satisfying it may be to boot a whining philosopher or lock one in a closet, there is a nagging difficulty left unresolved. It is laughably easy to dismiss out of hand the implication that, with their imperfect knowledge and jury-rigged categories, managers ought to suffer, ex officio, a fatal case of Hamletlike indecision. But it is not—or should not be—so easy to assume that they have direct, firm, and reliable knowledge of the world. They may act as if they do, often brilliantly, but that is not the same thing. In the still watches of the night—or when events call comfortable assumptions into question—we are only too nakedly aware of the difference. For a host of perfectly legitimate reasons, not least the desire to get on with things, we shun the melancholy Dane as a role model and choose to act as if our approximations of knowledge were firm enough to bear our weight. Career advancement in the Fortune 500 tends not to beset those who, like our nearer contemporary Mr. Prufrock, worry endlessly about the proper way to wear their trouser bottoms. To survive, let alone prosper, as managers, we must behave as if the maps we carry with us are reasonably accurate guides to real places. Current sales figures tell us something of value about what is really going on "out there." Inventory data describe actual changes in actual operations. Cost accounting systems make visible what it genuinely costs us to produce a widget.

Or do they? Certainly, there are bad figures, data, and systems, and good ones. The bad ones we discount; the good ones we trust: They are reliable maps, structures that will bear our weight. Of necessity we treat them as if they were second cousins to Gibraltar, rock solid and kickable at need. At some level, of course, we know better. In practice, though, we forget.

Left alone, however, these unstable pyramids of approximation readily turn into the kind of hard outcroppings on which we think it safe and sensible to build. As Robert Hayes and Kim Clark of Harvard Business School have found in their studies of manufacturing operations, direct labor may account for only a tiny fraction of production costs but often attracts the lion's share of management time, attention, and resources. At one high-tech company, managers used technically advanced scanners to monitor the work of line operators on a minute-to-minute basis. Those very managers, however, could not say how many manufacturing engineers represented nearly a quarter of total costs, as opposed to the 5 percent or so represented by direct labor.

At another company, where the value (in current dollars) of one plant's output ranged between $45 and $70 million a year during an eight-year period, the real value of that output (in constant dollars) showed a fairly sharp and regular decline. When Hayes and Clark brought these figures to the attention of the plant's managers, they found them hard to believe. The reason: They had come to think of the facility as a "$50 million plant" and so trusted the accounting system that told them, again and again, that such was indeed the case.[3]

These numbers are, at best, a rough proxy for what we genuinely want to know. In order to function at all, however, we treat them as if they told us the kinds of things we want them to—in much the same way that we easily come to treat statistical abstractions as having a different, more concrete kind of reality than they actually do. When a major producer of electronics equipment got serious some years back about improving the quality of its products, it informed all its component suppliers that it would expect a defect level of two parts per thousand. Along with the next 1000-piece shipment from a Japanese supplier came a note saying that, although it found the request puzzling, the company had wrapped the two defective units separately and included them in the shipment. Was this all right?

Yes, this is a funny moment in the annals of component sourcing, but it sketches out a process that happens all the time. Rules of thumb and working assumptions— handy devices with which to establish categories and divide up the world—quickly become for us descriptors of how the world really is. After a while, the tacit decision to treat our approximations this way becomes routine. Later still, even the fact of routine gets forgotten. Like carbon under great pressure for long periods of time, a handful of "as if" approximations will crystallize into the hard stone of fact. Hold one of these gems up to the light, and all you see is the crystal. The approximations, long forgotten, are invisible.

The Disappearance of Artifice

This process happens all the time and in all sorts of unlikely places. Just think, for example, about the language that we use daily. Turns of phrase that now roll off the tongue as uncomplicated, literal expressions were once metaphors lively enough to catch attention up short. There was a time when such phrases as the "tail of a kite" or a "river bed" or the "foot of a bed" were sufficiently novel and striking to change the way people saw things. Or when to speak of a situation as being "in a shambles" carried with it all the visceral associations of the slaughterhouse. Or when the decision to label as "equity" the certificates of participation in joint-stock company prompted nods of recognition at old legal and philosophical traditions. But that time passes. Left to itself, language builds up the way coral does. Living things die and leave their hard skeletons behind.

In institutional settings, the process is less spontaneous, less accidental, and so harsher. With a kind of remorseless geological pressure, time, usage, and familiarity squeeze out novelty, the consciousness of approximation, and leave not inert skeletons, but apparently crystalline facts behind. Just think for a moment of what happens to subtle new ideas as they make their way into the lexicon of management.

A worthy effort to get managers to pay close attention to the softer, nonquantitative or structural aspects of organizational life leads to a focus on corporate culture. So far, so good. As attention to culture grows, however, all the richness of the concept, all the careful understandings built up by generations of anthropological study, simply evaporate. Treating a company as if it were a society makes excellent sense—if done with a light touch and an appreciation of how far to push the analogy. But the inevitable juggernaut of seminar, training program, business media, consulting service, and graduate school curriculum tramples such niceties in the dust. And when

an enlightened CEO calls an underling aside and says,
"I've read Peters and Waterman, and I want a new culture in my organization by Monday morning," all is lost
beyond recall.

Or take the current fascination with productivity improvement. Facing severe competitive challenge, American managers have at last gotten it into their heads that
they can no longer rest content with inefficient operations. Who can or would argue with so reasonable a
determination or so timely a commitment of energy and
resources? But when boosting productivity comes to
mean in practice nothing more than an efficiency-driven
effort to cut costs and do better with line workers what is
now being done, we can watch the coral build up before
our very eyes. In an earlier environment, the link between old-fashioned, direct labor-based productivity and
competitive strength was obvious and immediate. Today, that linkage is more complicated and less certain.
Doing the right things is every bit as important as doing
things right. Time was, we could think of direct-labor
productivity as a pretty fair approximation of competi-
tiveness and be confident we were on the mark. No
longer. The proxy does not hold. Forgetful that it was—
and is—but a proxy that holds for some circumstances
but not all, many of today's managers treat as a living fact
what is no more than the hard shell of past experience.

So it is with most of the maps by which managers
steer. What was once known to be an artifice, though no
less useful for that, gradually loses its air of being an
imaginatively constructed thing and, equally gradually,

takes on the air of being something real and hard and concrete in its own right. The clever ratio for measuring the behavior of inventory costs once prompted smiles of appreciation at its ingenuity. After a time, it becomes only another dry fact. More than that, it stops being a lens through which people look creatively at inventory and becomes, by tacit consent, a simple, true statement of the way inventory really is. It is no longer seen as an artifice, as something constructed, but as a solid chunk of data, as a rock upon which to build. Later, when it has become so commonplace, so obvious, as to seem a child's plaything, it makes its home in primers and textbooks somewhere between the alphabet and old wives' tales. Those of us who, for our sins, have taught English composition to college sophomores who very much wished to be elsewhere remember at least one student complaining about how familiar and cliché-ridden Shakespeare was.

There is a great temptation to smile knowingly at such complaints, but only when other people are making them. It is harder to force a grin when the silliness is ours. Back in the 1960s and 1970s, remember, innumerable managers came to worship the formal techniques of strategic planning as if they were pieces of the true cross. This idolization of experience curves, growth share matrices, and portfolio concepts got more than a few companies into trouble—not because the techniques were worthless (in fact, they were and are of real value) but because their value lay in being used as stimulators of, not replacements for, hard thinking. According to Fred

Gluck, a colleague and director of McKinsey & Company, "the problem was that the techniques became venerated for their own sake. Processes, black boxes, and rituals were formalized in an attempt to make strategy objective, but only succeeded in making it mechanical."

Here, again, we can see the awareness of artifice giving way to the celebration of apparent fact without any thought for the likely consequences. Albert North Whitehead, the noted philosopher, had a term for this all-too-common mental reflex: he called it "the fallacy of misplaced concreteness." Treating an abstract construct—say, the notion of an experience curve—as if it were an elementary crystal of fact is just the kind of attribution of false concreteness Whitehead had in mind. The point is not that to think of experience curves or other constructs in this manner is an empty exercise barren of utility. Far from it. It may be exceptionally helpful to do so. It is terribly important to know how to categorize the needs and opportunities of our coffee business. The problems start when we forget that that *is* what we are doing, when we forget the "as if" quality of the conceptual tools we use.

Much as workmen put a scaffold in place before tackling the construction job at hand, we need a support on which to stand while we do our thinking. The workmen do not confuse their scaffold with what they are building. Nor do they forget that the building on which they are working is something "built," something constructed, not something that has always been there in its present form. Neither should we. But we do, repeatedly.

In fact, it is the rare occasion when we do not. For the most part, we fashion our ideas out of material that will suit the taste of the organizational context for which those ideas are intended. Does the boss like to hear three possible courses of action discussed before a recommendation gets offered? Well, every circumstance will miraculously have three viable options. Does the executive committee frown on budget requests that pay little attention to cost savings? Well, every proposal will seem the offspring of an unrepentant Scrooge. Are we actively aware of how these preconditions structure thought? Yes, perhaps, at the outset, but less so as our mode of thinking becomes a reflex, a habit encouraged and rewarded. After a while, that reflex will seem the most natural thing in the world.

The successful artifice tends not to call attention to itself; its seeming transparency is no small part of what made it successful in the first place. How, then, to be aware of its presence, how not to forget? Before all else, the consciousness of artifice in particular settings depends upon a general sense of the world's "constructed" quality—that is, upon a reversal of the normal way we look at things. Rather than assume that facts are "there" in the nature of things unless proved otherwise, we ought to start from an assumption of their artificial quality. That way, we remind ourselves continually that the stuff in which we deal is "built" stuff. If it is useful, well and good; if not, we have a leg up on knowing how it skews and conditions our thought.

Looking back on the early years of strategic fervor, Gluck notes that

> I own an artifact of those times—a wheel of strategy. It's a little like those wheels that tell you which color to paint your walls, or give you your horoscope, but I like to think of it as a prayer wheel. You set your return on assets—the middle wheel—at the real market growth rate on the outer wheel. Then you turn the inner wheel to an arrow on the middle wheel corresponding to your share of the market. Finally, you look through a little slot on the inner wheel—where it reads "Strategic Action to Take"—and read one of six basic strategies: "invest," "protect," "improve," "maintain," "cash out," or "critical review." Oh, yes, there's a little note on the back in small type that says, "The actions indicated by the Strategy Guide may need to be adjusted under special circumstances."[4]

With a prayer wheel of this sort, as any 10-K will attest, there can be no salvation by faith alone. All the murky subtleties with which managers struggle daily, all the quirks of this or that market, of this or that customer or vendor—all the "special circumstances" that give life to the distinct environment in which each company must operate—are here smuggled into the equation through the small type on the back.

Like the world-weary student's disappointment with Shakespeare, this bundling in of paying guests through the service entrance brings a smile. But we smile, for the most part, at the wrong sin. The trouble with the prayer wheel of strategy is not that its categories pay only the most discreet lip service to the booming confusion of the environment in which managers function. So obvious an omission readily calls attention to itself and is therefore venial—or just plain sophomoric. The trouble lies, instead, with the way in which those categories get thought about in the first place. They lurk in the mind as real, concrete things when in fact they are no more than the fragile "built" remnants of long trains of "as if" thinking. Long familiarity has made their coral-like nature invisible to the casual observer who, not expecting artifice, does not see it or sense it. But these categories are not naturally occurring phenomena like mountains or flowers or antelope. They *are* an artifice, a man-made construct from which the organic "as if" has leached (or been purged) over time.

We forget, in our language as in the circumstances of our daily lives, how completely, how utterly, we are surrounded by such "built" remnants. Not only is there unsuspected artifice all about us; our very relation to the main points of reference in our world is itself a built thing. We find it hard to imagine, for example, that access to knowledge of something as basic as the calendar can in any way be privileged, that it can represent a property right that is closely guarded and sparingly shared. Yet it can be—and has been. In China of the Sung Dynasty, the calendar was not a set of neutral facts put together according to the best astronomic and scientific knowledge. It was not an objective reality equally available to all people, a set of universal reference points. Nothing of the sort. "In China," as David Landes remarks in his history of clockmaking, the calendar was a perquisite of sovereignty, like the right to mint coins. Knowledge of the right time and season was power, for it was this knowledge that governed both the acts of everyday life and the decisions of state. Each emperor inaugurated his reign with the promulgation of this calendar, often different from the one that had preceded it. His court astronomers were the only persons who were permitted in principle to use timekeeping and astronomical instruments or to engage in astronomical study. His time was China's time.[5]

Today, the press often reminds us, especially when it has come in for a nasty bout of criticism, that many nations do not enjoy a free press and that we should cherish the one we have. This makes sense to us as a general caution because we know quite well that many societies exist in which information is not freely available, in which governments actively manage what knowledge the public may have. We know, too, that such nations regard the dissemination of facts or opinions not officially sanctioned as a subversive activity of the first order. We know all this because it is a recognizable, if repugnant, part of our world. We fancy that we would know how to read a Soviet newspaper or listen to an Eastern Bloc radio broadcast. We have even learned to keep a large salt cellar at our elbow when we plow through the celebrity gossip in our local tabloids. We can imagine that the best, most accurate news is not a universally available commodity. But we have a hard time imagining a world like Sung China in which free access to the calendar is off limits, in which knowledge of the seasons is privileged— in which such knowledge could be "built" differently or treated as private property or found to be wrong or biased.

To keep from going crazy, we learn over time to treat many of the constructs about us as if they were as firm as the chunks of the earth's mantle on which we stand. Put mildly, if we had to start from scratch every day, we would not get a whole lot done. Some certainties, at least some functional certainties, are essential if we are to do any more than survive as protoplasm survives. But do we know, say, how long an inch is—not as a practical matter but as an ultimate issue of measurement? Do we really know more about the length of that inch than the Sung Chinese did about when summer was? Do we know how long an hour is? Did we always think of it as having the duration it has now? Just how "given" in the nature of things are all the little constructed items we take for granted?

The uncomfortable answer is, Not very. Consider the hour as a unit of time. Before the middle decades of the fourteenth century, an hour was not the standardized mixture of television programming and commercials we have come to know. Nor were there necessarily twenty-four of them in a day. Nor did the hours that did exist have to measure out at equal lengths. In the early life of the Church, the day was divided by a series of canonical or devotional hours, but their number depended on local custom. Even in the sixth century, when that number was fixed at seven, the precise time (in our sense) for each depended on geographical location and on the season.

By the midyears of the fourteenth century, when the lay keeping of time had fixed the length of a day at twenty-four hours of equal duration, the first hour began not upon the stroke of midnight but upon the stroke of noon. There was, moreover, a long stretch of time before then during which the number of hours in a day had been established at twenty-four but their need to be of equal length had not. If the periods of daylight and dark had a total of twelve hours each, then an hour's duration would inevitably reflect the vagaries of location and season.

The length of an hour, then, is not a self-evident matter of fact. It is, rather, the virtually archaeological result of custom, practice, and discovery in many cultures over several millennia. So, too, the minute, which derives from an ancient Babylonian measure for one-sixtieth of a unit and which did not get applied to a subdivision of the hour until the thirteenth century or so. Not only that, both represent the application to time of units initially devised for other reasons, like the measurement of distance. The Egyptians, as Daniel Boorstin tells us in his account of our discovery of time, probably measured their day in twenty-four hours (of unequal length) because their numerical system, derived from the Babylonians, was based on multiples of the number six. Thus, Boorstin concludes,

when we mark each hour of our 24-hour day, and designate the minutes after the hour, we are living, as a historian of ancient science reminds us, by "the results of a Hellenistic modification of an Egyptian practice combined with Babylonian numerical procedures."[6]

Perhaps, after all, we are not so very different from the Sung Chinese. Much of the world around us, even those portions we think of as solid and given in the nature of things, is a human construct of mixed provenance. It did not have to be—and often was not—the way it is now. There is no natural law that requires a week to have seven days or even mandates that a unit of time like the week should exist in the first place. No shaping logic of the galaxy established that a pound should weigh what it does or a foot cover thus and such a distance or an acre so much ground. The year in which George Washington was born began not on the first of January but on the twenty-fifth of March. No decree of nature stipulated that when men came to draw maps of their world, they would place north at the top. What we understand by these measurements and directions did not spring full blown out of nature the way a rainbow does. They are "built" things, constructs, archaeological relics. And being man-made out of shreds and patches over time, man can control them the way Chinese emperors did the calendar—or can try.

For managers, the man-made quality of so much of their professional apparatus holds a special lesson. Charged with acting under pressure of time in complex environments, they must be quickly able to tell which of the factors about them are really beyond their control and which are amenable to change—that is, which are levers, and which are constraints. Is the hurdle rate for new capital investments a fixed, elementary part of the landscape, or is it a fragile approximation that does not really catch meaningful dimensions of performance? The lesson here, of course, is that a persistent awareness of artifice is the best over-the-counter remedy we have against being made the unwary prisoners of our own assumptions, concepts, and techniques. As with the prayer wheel of strategy, it is the underlying categories—the conventions of thought—that matter.

II

The hidden operations of such categories and conventions do much to shape the environment in which managers function. When their awareness of artifice disappears, there are real-world consequences to be faced. Years ago, two scientists in GE's research laboratory discovered an intriguing new monomer-based adhesive material, called Anaerobic Permafil, which bonded parts together quite effectively—but only in the absence of air. GE marketed the product for a while by selling the basic monomer along with instructions on how to turn it into the adhesive substance. GE could not sell the adhesive itself through regular commercial channels because the substance had to be continuously exposed to a steady flow of oxygen. In practice, this meant keeping its container linked to an air compressor. Were the oxygen supply cut off, it would polymerize where it sat.

Not surprisingly, these limitations kept the adhesive from becoming a great success and ultimately prompted GE to get out of the business. As long as managers viewed the appeal of the product as being inescapably constrained by the bulk of an air compressor, their decision made perfect sense. They did not, of course, press the laboratory to try to make the adhesive less sensitive to oxygen because that would diminish its attractive properties. Their problem was clear, and their decision to get out of the business reasonable.

There was, however, another way to think about the problem. What if, instead of making the adhesive less sensitive to oxygen, it was possible to increase its sensitivity enormously—say, by a factor of one thousand? In that case, the adhesive could be stored fully prepared in polyethylene bottles, which allow some oxygen to pass through, and be distributed as a regular industrial product. In fact, a chemical process for boosting oxygen sensitivity did exist, and an adhesive of severely limited commercial appeal became the cornerstone of the new Loctite Corporation.[7]

As this little tale suggests, problem definition, whether in R&D or in any other corporate function, is as much a "built" thing or construct as is our notion of an hour's duration or the proper location of north on a map. Managers respond to the circumstances in which they find themselves by defining, explicitly or not, the nature of the issues or problems with which they must wrestle. Only then do they bring to bear the appropriate resources, formal methods of analysis, and techniques.

First they must know *how* to think about what lies in front of them, and that mode of knowing is always deeply influenced by the underlying conventions in and through which they think. Depending on what they see the issue to be, they will bring to bear this or that line of response. But first they must *see* the issue to be a certain kind of thing—that is, they must categorize it, give it a label, find out where it fits in the larger scheme of things.

The same is true of our own daily lives. We may have fairly good control over what we think, but we are much less the masters of how we think. We may see the world clearly through the lenses of our eyeglasses; but if we have worn them for a long time, we often forget we have them on. A refracted view is how we come to think things really look. So much is common sense, even if uncomfortable common sense. Less easy to remember is that, if managers ask about the commercial possibilities of an adhesive linked to an air compressor for storage, they have already shaped and constrained the answer.

Now, consider the story of a different adhesive. Back in the early 1950s, the Tennessee Eastman Company was experimenting with new kinds of tough, heat-resistant materials out of which to fabricate jet plane canopies. One young chemist, Fred Joyner, wanted to measure the refractive index of a particular monomer on which he had been working. Here is what happened:

He put a thin film of this monomer between the closely-fitting faces of the two prisms of an Abbe refractometer. After the measurement was made and recorded, Fred was unable to separate the prisms. He took his problem to his laboratory supervisor, Dr. Newt Shearer, but nothing they could think of freed the prisms. Finally, Fred and Newt came to me to report that they ruined a $700 instrument. Any concern I had about the refractometer was swept away by the sudden realization that what we had was not a useless instrument, but a unique adhesive. Serendipity had given me a second chance but this time the mental process led to inspiration.

A second chance? H. W. Coover, whose account this is, had worked during World War II for the Kodak Research Laboratories in Rochester, where he experimented with the same monomer as a possible material for making precision gunsight lenses. It had some attractive properties for this use but proved a dead end because it "stuck to everything [it] touched." As Coover puts it, "I was thinking gunsights, and nothing but gunsights and the adhesive qualities of these monomers were a serious obstacle in my path." This time around, however, he was prepared to look beyond the immediate problem to an entirely different kind of possibility.[8]

Conventions of thought—those subtle, often taken-for-granted assumptions that give structure to the way we view things—are much harder to make visible, to put on the table for discussion, than are explicit ideas or items of knowledge. If pressed, we can probably say whether we think a particular court decision was fair or identify the person who signed the Emancipation Proclamation. If we have not heard enough about the court decision to form a judgment, or if we do not know about this aspect of Lincoln's presidency, we can readily con-

fess that we are out of our depth. We know we do not
know. But if the question facing us is *why* do we think
such and such a decision was fair or *why* are we so confident it was Lincoln, our response will be less immediate and, perhaps, less certain. Further, if pushed to say
aloud *how* it is we think about the notion of fairness to
begin with or about the canons of historical evidence, we
will likely have a harder time still. We are not sure how
we know what we know.

In the cases of both industrial adhesives discussed
above, conventions initially defined—although they did
not ultimately control—how the situation at hand was
understood. As with our knowledge of Lincoln's proclamation and our opinions of a court's wisdom, unvoiced
expectations about the nature of a problem or about the
relevant properties of a new material did much to condition how each got thought of. Like fishermen of an
earlier time, we cast our nets deep, often by reflex and
habit. All we know of what lies under the surface is what
a net's fluidly changing shape, well out of sight, drags
up. When we think about it, we remember that all we
have landed is a partial catch. But we do not think about
it all that much. Or about how the forgotten shape and
movement of the net condition what it brings to the
surface. We forget the artifice, the conventions.

The Role of Convention

Conventions do not simply emerge out of the air as cos-
mic rays do. They are "built" things, man-made, and

have a history. They structure meaning, and the less obvious they are, the more subtly they will do their work. The further out of sight they operate, the less visible their trappings, the more thoroughly forgotten their nature as construct—in short, the greater their surface transparency, the stronger their power will be to control, condition, and predispose. As with the once-live metaphors in phrases like a "riverbed" or the "tail of a kite" or with the archaeological character of our calendar and units of time, so with the operation of conventions generally: Over time, our awareness of their artifice evaporates, leaving behind a residue that seems utterly matter-of-fact. It is this surface transparency, this invisibility, that gives conventions their special force in human affairs—in the *how* of how we think. Our culture has long known the power of unseen gods.

Sometimes they take strange forms. As late as the mid-1940s, the standard product of the American recording industry was the 78 rpm shellac disc. Better than nothing, of course, but far from a pleasant or faithful reproduction of the original sound. The distortions and short-playing times of these records may seem inconceivable in a popular product to a generation that has grown up on the marvels of Japanese consumer electronics, but then they represented the state of the art.

Peter Goldmark, later the president of CBS Laboratories, got organizational support from CBS toward the end of 1945 to work on an idea he had for taking a "systems approach" to the development of a modern long-playing record. The systems approach was essential, Goldmark thought, because the quality and duration of a recording depended not on a single, but on a series of technical elements and decisions. It was his idea to experiment with the whole system. As he tells the story, "I proposed to change a number of things—the amplifier, the material of the record, the shape of the groove, the cartridge and stylus, the method of recording, [and] the turntable drive. . . ."

This Goldmark did, substituting vinyl for shellac, finding ways to cut the grooves finer and finer, and so on. Still, problems remained with the quality of sound. Every piece of the system received his attention except the microphone, which the industry regarded as being nearly perfect as it was. As so often happens, what everyone knows is not worth knowing, and what everyone swears by is often worth swearing at. There was, it turned out, a real problem with the microphone (it was vulnerable to phase distortion), and Goldmark had to hunt down a German company that was beginning to produce a new kind of condenser microphone that avoided these difficulties.

Finally came the anticipated problems of transferring the contents of the old 78 discs onto discs of the new format. Careful electronic timing, with the help of an oscillator, allowed for transcription without the ear being able to tell where the gaps had been. Some problems, however, had not been anticipated. According to Goldmark,

We played it again and again until we could make the syn-
chronization as acceptable to our ears as possible. After a while
I could tell almost by instinct where there was a splice. Then
one day a new problem arose. When making the original recording on the 78, the orchestra would record in 4-minute
sessions but they would spread them over a period of several
days. Consequently, the pitch of the orchestra would not be
consistent over the entire movement, and we found that in
splicing we had two different sounds from the same orchestra.[9]

Two points here are worth noting. First, the technical
community within which Goldmark functioned shared a
host of assumptions about the way things worked and
why. Some were easily and immediately visible, like the
part of an iceberg that shows above water, but others lay
well below the surface. The initial resistance he encoun-
tered from top-level executives (the head of Columbia
Records suggested, kindly, that he drop the whole idea
and try his hand at something related to television), hard
facts about the industry's economics (who would want to
render obsolete huge investments in plant and equipment to press shellac records?), and the lack of any systematic knowledge of the relevant technologies (virtually
none of the science had been done in an organized fashion)—all this worked to create an environment in which
it was hard to conceive the possibility of significant and
radical change. More to the point, in such an environment, maintained as it was by people who think their
view of things eminently reasonable given the facts, casual trial-and-error observations—like the assumption of
the microphone's perfection—readily become hard-and-

fast certainties. To the inhabitants of Main Street, Joe's barbershop down on Third is, without doubt, the best barbershop in the world.

The task of charting out new territory involves not just learning how to survey and make sense of what was previously unknown. Far more difficult is learning how to see what is really there and not what the conventional wisdom suggests is there. In a sense, we see what we are prepared to see. The real problem, of course, is that the preparation largely takes place invisibly, out of sight. On the surface, accepted categories rule—and give up their sway most reluctantly. Indeed, as Boorstin interprets early efforts to draw accurate maps of the world,

> the great obstacle to discovering the shape of the earth, the continents, and the ocean was not ignorance but the illusion of knowledge. Imagination drew in bold strokes, instantly serving hopes and fears, while knowledge advanced by slow increments and contradictory witnesses. Villagers who themselves feared to ascend the mountain-tops located their departed ones on the impenetrable heavenly heights.[10]

The "illusion of knowledge" is a very determined adversary, not least because it relies for much of its force on the hidden effects of convention. To be effective, conventions must be shared, and the staying power of beliefs that are the common property of the groups in which we live and work is considerable. We believe, everyone believes, that technical difficulties cannot be the fault of the microphone because, as we all know, the microphone is perfect. To unwarranted assumption gets added the great energy of social pressure. The combination is hard to resist.

The second point worth noting about this story is that even when Goldmark was sufficiently able to pierce through convention to identify a remaining problem (inconsistency of pitch), the key to understanding what was the matter lay not in further technical analysis but in knowing something about how the recordings had been made. In other words, there were specific and unique facts about those recordings (facts that did not *have* to be that way) that Goldmark could know only by knowing something of their history, how they came to be. There was no way to guess, in the abstract, that orchestras had recorded in four-minute sessions over a period of days. Yet if that had not been the case, then the unwanted changes in pitch would have had to come from as yet undiscovered glitches in the technical system. Finding out what those glitches were would then have dominated the agenda for technical work. Only by knowing a particular, unique, and historical fact about those recordings could the researchers allocate their efforts wisely.

Individual Facts

Even in the face of social usage and the passage of time, individual facts—the precise data of history—matter. They are, in fact, the main instrument of artifice. Time inevitably glosses over the particularities of each situation or circumstance, and this slow erosion of focus is what makes it possible for conventions and categories to

operate unseen. Adding the facts back calls a halt to this
silent process. Ferreting out specific, relevant detail dis-
rupts the mechanics of erosion, which need inattention
and forgetfulness to do their work.

In the 1790s a yellow fever epidemic struck Philadelphia, and medical opinion about its cause broke down
pretty much along party lines. Doctors of Federalist af-
filiation thought the disease must be the result of some
foreign-produced and imported contagion, Republican
physicians, the result of some local corruption of the soil.
There is no way to make any sense out of this odd diag-
nostic lock-step unless we know that there was another
great fever disturbing the world at that time, the French
Revolution, and that men of a Federalist turn of mind
were deeply distrustful of its political infection being
carried to these shores. For their part, Republicans were
perfectly willing to believe things were already rotten
enough at home. That particular division of opinion was
not the way things had to be; it was simply the way they
were.

Nearly a century later, utopian fiction was all the
rage—books written about nearly every form of utopia
imaginable, perfect societies based on human compas-
sion, engineering principles, robust exercise, nutritional
crackers, or some combination of these ingredients. One
of the most popular, Edward Bellamy's *Looking Backward*, offered its readers a vision of a glorious future in
which the evils of grimy industrialization had been overcome and people talked with each other mostly by telephone. Why so great an allegiance to Mr. Bell's wondrous

invention? Not, it turns out, because they were mesmer-
ized by the new technology but, instead, because the
germ theory of disease had begun to receive wide attention. Many people were afraid, understandably so, of
infectious agents too small to see with the naked eye,
and so they much preferred the safety of a telephone
conversation to prolonged contact with large groups of
their neighbors. The reason for their curious preference
did not have to be that way, but it was.

At a theoretical level, there is no way to predict that clas-
sical orchestras, in the days of 78 rpm recordings, would
perform their music in four-minute stretches. Like the
doctors of late eighteenth-century Philadelphia or the
happy denizens of Boston in the year 2000, these collections of musicians acted as they did for reasons at which
a proverbial newly landed Martian could not hope to
guess. To understand the consequences of their actions,
we must know something specific about them, something
historical. We must be able to tell *why* everyone seems to
think the butler did it.

Especially when artifice leaches out, leaving only conventions behind, we must know the right facts to add back.
As one historian has nicely put it, "Economists . . . tend
to set policy by averages, not by exceptions. . . . But history never repeats itself exactly, and the historian is best
equipped to point this out." To know why France was sym-
pathetic to free trade in 1848 but backed away in 1873, we
must not resort to theories of cycles, sunspots, or self-cor-
recting markets. We must know instead that "Louis Napoleon Bonaparte was trained in England as a free-trader

and that during that period he was the guy at the top."[11]

Idiosyncratic facts do much to explain what is, as well as what is possible. Even so, our tendency to find our way through the world by unthinking reliance on "as if" maps continues largely unabated. Every now and then, a word about the precise nature of Louis Napoleon Bonaparte's economic training may bring us up short, but we tend to ignore that word, if possible, or if not, to pay it only the most limited attention. As a rule, the more systematic the explanation—sunspots, imported germs, a glitch in recording technology—the more comfortable we are. Curious individual facts are, by contrast, a source of pointed discomfort. They work to show us things, people, and circumstances in their full and unrelieved singularity. They require dealing with. They punch a hole in the bottom of otherwise watertight formulas. Like a selective chemical dye, they fasten themselves immediately and indelibly to the remnants of artifice and so make it impossible for us to pretend that all artifice has evaporated long ago. Like some textbookish economists, we prefer to operate and interpret by averages and extrapolations, not by exceptions or historical singularities.

The Science Center, a major Harvard University building designed by José Luis Sert, has far more architectural detail at one end than the other. A carefully rendered intention? Hardly. As someone who worked in Sert's office at the time recalls, there was

a huge cardboard model of the proposed Science Center [that] stood in Sert's drafting room, oriented in such a way that the

Littauer end [the one more richly developed] faced the door. Sert would enter the room and immediately begin working on that model at its nearest point. The side of the model hardest to reach was the long side facing north, and in the finished building this shows the least elaboration.[12]

Now this is not to argue that the *only* things that matter are such one-off singularities. Far from it. Without broader maps and more inclusive categories, we would never get anywhere. There is not enough time in one person's life to discover through firsthand experience whether every wooden match in creation will light when struck. The problem comes when, eager to get the lowdown on matches, we forget that the kind of general knowledge we are working with stands at several removes from the particularities of unique instances of match lighting. It is not the fact of conventions that troubles, but our tendency not to see conventions for what they are. As all good economists know, averages are fine—so long as we remember that they *are* averages, statistical creations, pieces of deliberate artifice. So long as we remember that they are "built" things.

Still, we are uncomfortable with singular facts. Think, for instance, how different the relations of size and shape are for insects than they are for us. As Stephen Jay Gould reminds us, geometry mandates that surface area increases more slowly than does volume. Consequently,

An insect performs no miracle in walking up a wall or upon the surface of a pond; the small gravitational force pulling it down or under is easily counteracted by surface adhesion. . . .

The relative weakness of gravitational forces also permits a mode of growth that large animals could not maintain. Insects have an external skeleton and can grow only by discarding it and secreting a new one to accommodate the enlarged body. For a period between shedding and regrowth, the body must remain soft. A large mammal without any supporting structures would collapse to a formless mass. . . .[13]

The evolution of architecture shows many of these same principles at work. In the days before illumination by electricity and structural steel, it was simply not possible to build a large medieval cathedral to the same design—and in the same proportions—as a smaller (and broader) parish church. "The inside of such a cathedral," Gould writes, "would have been darker than the deed of Judas." After all, "medieval churches, like tapeworms, lacked internal systems and must alter their shape to produce more external surface as they are made larger. . . . Theological motives may have dictated the position of . . . [the transepts], but the laws of size required their presence."[14]

Science fiction mavens seem not to have learned this lesson. Monstrous creatures like giant flying ants many feet in length are not impossible to imagine because no genetic mutation could have tested things out in this direction. They are impossible—like certain cathedral designs—in old-fashioned terms. Most of the terrifying apparitions at which we quiver in late-night reruns frighten us because of their horrifying, if unlikely, plausibility. Maybe no such thing ever really existed, but we believe that it could, and that infinitesimal grain of possibility rivets us to our seats. Truth is often stranger than fiction, and who knows what unseemly aberrations a healthy dose of radiation might cause in this or that otherwise familiar creature?

What we forget in these imaginings is that we make such grants of plausibility on the basis of implicit extrapolations. (Elsewhere, we fashion our categories on other bases, other principles of relation.) Well, if an ant of normal size can do thus and such, think what it would be like if it were a hundred times larger, or a thousand. Communal shudder. The emotional mechanism is perfectly legitimate and often quite effective. The process of extrapolation—of categorization—that supports it is not. A specious aura of plausibility blinds us to nagging, inescapable, and singular facts about the relation of volume to size.

The "as-if-ness" of these unthinking grants of plausibility do more than condition our late-night viewing habits or influence the way we make sense of nineteenth-century French trade policy, the causes of yellow fever, or the limitations of old 78 rpm recordings. They also limit—in a corporate environment—the way managers think about many things, as, for example, the allowable dimensions of change in products and processes. Alterations in scale and complexity do not simply require—or allow—building the same thing in the same way, only a bit larger or smaller. Market competition and technical necessity no more follow the rule of straight geometric extrapolation than nature does. If the passenger ships of today were just proportionally larger versions of those of a century ago, they would no more stay afloat than gigantic ants can fly. If the floor plan of Chartres had followed the proportions of many earlier parish churches, it would have long been a pile of rubble.

The technical systems on which modern products and processes depend follow a logic of development that makes sense only within certain parameters of size and complexity, and there is nothing for it but to know in each case just what those parameters are. Build a large dam out of the same material successfully used in a much smaller one, and wise people will quickly move away— lock, stock, and barrel—from the path of the inevitable flood. Build a high-performance automobile engine out of the same material used for a power motor, and the car is not going to finish the Indy 500. Build a DC-10's airframe and wings out of the same material the Wright brothers used, and it is not going to get off the ground.

"Large machines," as an expert on technological innovation cautions, "require materials of comparatively higher strength-to-weight ratios. Similarly, special alloys are almost always needed to ensure sufficient penetration of heat when manufacturing large steel parts. Such a need does not arise for smaller parts."[15] Changes in overall scale—whether of religious buildings, passenger shops, late-night insects, or consumer goods—necessarily lead to other, related changes in internal proportion, material, shape, complexity, and so on. No simple extrapolation will do here, no formulaic "as if." What happens, though, when unthinking formulas, blind categories, still carry the day? Nothing good.

Contemplate for a moment, in this light, the recent experience of the American automobile industry. When in the 1960s it first began to worry seriously about the competitive threat posed by foreign imports, it turned its considerable energies toward the design and production of small cars that would more than hold their own with those from Germany and later Japan. As a strategic decision, this commitment made excellent sense; as a practical matter, it turned into a holy mess. Responsible managers went about their design and production tasks under the assumption that making good small cars meant making little big cars—and doing it well. The "as if" virus quickly reached epidemic proportions in Detroit, although few of those stricken with it initially had any awareness that things were not as they should be.

Here, in one version, is part of what happened:

> Chevrolet engineers took the prototype Vega to the GM test track in Milford, Michigan. After eight miles, the front of the Vega broke off. The front end of the car separated from the rest of the vehicle. It must have set a record for the shortest time taken for a new car to fall apart. The car was sent to Chevy engineering, where the front end was beefed up. Already the small, svelte American answer to foreign car craftsmanship was putting on weight—20 pounds in understructure to hold the front end intact. Thus began a fattening up process of the "less-than-2,000-pound" mini-car that would take it to ponderous proportions in weight and price compared to the original car described [by top management].[16]

The point, of course, is not that adding structural support is an inappropriate way to solve the problem of readily detachable front ends. It is, rather, that following such an approach for a subcompact car is to treat it as if it were merely a pint-sized version of an old V-8 road cruiser, which it surely is not. In order to know which design changes really are needed, it is first necessary to understand how a small car's various systems and structures fit and work together. What is the "logic" that holds them, what special peculiarities and relationships are essential, what constraints are unavoidable—these are the sorts of questions Detroit was (and still is) slow in learning to ask.

To repeat, idiosyncratic facts—the things that get lost when awareness of artifice disappears—matter. And they matter not only in themselves but also in their effect on what we are prepared—and thus able—to see. When scientists first discovered in Africa the fossil remains that irrefutably linked *Homo sapiens* to our ancestors among the apes, many observers refused to see these so-called australopithecines for what they were because, although they obviously walked erect, their brains were much smaller than those of humans. Looking back on that episode, Gould tells us that "we must ascribe this 'spectacular failure' primarily to a subtle prejudice that led to the following, invalid extrapolation: We dominate other animals by brain power (and little else); therefore, an increasing brain must have propelled our own evolution at all stages."[17] To read this critical evidence correctly, we must be able to see that a bunch of bones in Africa tells an evolutionary story unlike the one we expected to hear, unlike the one suggested by convention. But it is a plausible story nonetheless. A different kind of sense is not nonsense but sense of a different and often unexpected kind.

Seeing it means seeing the facts on which it rests for what they are. Fossil men inevitably raise questions of interpretation, whether at Olduvai Gorge or at a Detroit test track. Or, for that matter, at a small engineering company in India. Peter Drucker tells the story this way:

> Shortly after World War II, a small Indian engineering firm bought the license to produce a European-designed bicycle with an auxiliary light engine. It looked like an ideal product for India; yet it never did well. The owner of this small firm noticed, however, that substantial orders came in for the engines alone. At first he wanted to turn down those orders; what could anyone possibly do with such a small engine? It was curiosity alone that made him go to the actual area the orders came from. There he found farmers were taking the engines off the bicycles and using them to power irrigation pumps that hitherto had been hand-operated. This manufacturer is now the world's largest maker of small irrigation pumps, selling them by the millions. His pumps have revolutionized farming all over Southeast Asia.[18]

Looked at from one direction, what the owner of the Indian firm did was what any good businessperson ought to be expected to do: identify the character of demand and, along with it, a new opportunity. In practice, this meant seeing the existence of a question to be answered where others might have just filled orders. Seeing that sort of question, however, turns out not to be quite so easy or obvious as it might initially seem, and grasping

the fact of an unanticipated opportunity, more difficult
still. Later chapters will speak more directly about methods likely to encourage such seeing and grasping. Here
the challenge is to recognize the need—and recognize it
clearly.

When facts do not neatly fit into the categories prepared for them, the usual impulse is to try to shove them
in without looking, the way a messy, last-minute traveler
crams odds and ends into a suitcase. In the face of real-
world pressures and facts that do not fit, few of us are
likely to remember how much of an artifice, a construct,
a thing "built" such categories are. For the most part, we
are happy enough to get the damned suitcase closed.

III

Jumping up and down this way about the "built" quality
of the world is not an idle exercise. Nor is an active bout
of finger-pointing at the ease with which we forget just
how convention- and category-ridden our experience of
that world is. Without such artifice, without maps of all
sorts, we would, of course, be truly lost and directionless.
The fact that we have them—are surrounded by them—
is, for the most part, a happy fact.

What is not happy is our tendency to deny or be un-
aware that they are precisely what we *do* have. And that
denial has serious consequences. Not only do we lose
over time our awareness of artifice; we respond badly to
suggestions that we need to recapture it. In a sense,
conventional wisdom—what everyone knows—is an un-

intentional conspiracy to keep such troubling, inconvenient material out of sight and out of mind. Worse, it is a conspiracy that relies heavily for its success on the well-tested dynamics of social pressure. No wonder the effort to add facts back often runs into such fierce resistance.

The Base of the Iceberg

Years ago, everyone knew that you could not sell packaged chocolate chip cookies through the grocery store or supermarket—that is, if those cookies were to taste at all the way the home-baked version did: crispy on the outside, chewy within. No matter how tight the seal on the package, the cookies would dry out and get hard all the way through. Putting satellite bakeries near retail outlets might help win this race against time, but the realities of shelf life and the poor economics of small-scale bakery operations argued against it. To be in the packaged chocolate chip cookie business, everyone knew you had to sell crumbly circular bricks. Well, everyone was wrong. Cookies get hard because their sugars crystallize, not because they dry out. If it were possible to build a composite, two-part cookie—a cookie with sugars that crystallize at different rates—and assemble it just before baking, the need for uneconomic satellite bakeries would disappear. And a staid old consumer business could be revitalized.

Years ago, everyone knew that American firms could

no longer hope to make any money in the steel business. Everyone knew that the most stable, least adventurous places to look for a predictable career and a steady paycheck were banking and the telephone industry. Everyone knew that American drivers would always flock to the rolling living rooms that Detroit turned out in such abundance. Everyone knew that higher demand for electricity would lead to constant technical progress and lower rates. Everyone knew that Chicago-based dry goods merchants would always live in a different competitive world from that of money center banks. Well, we say smugly, everyone was wrong. We would not be so smug if we were honest about how difficult it is to be right.

Like the Molière character who awoke one morning to discover he had been speaking prose all his life, we continually find that there are many sets of categories that still shape our thinking unawares—categories that we are reluctant to remember. When, for example, we read a biographical sketch about some current figure of interest, there are certain kinds of information that we fully expect the author to pass along in the nature of things. What does the person look like, for example? How does he or she act in this or that set of circumstances? What are the known facts about this individual's past? Where born? Into what sort of family? Where schooled? What types of jobs or activities? We would want to know about special accomplishments, psychological quirks, formative influences. Was there a particular teacher who made all the difference? A coach? A boss? And, of course, what is the subject like in person? Nothing out of the ordinary here, perfectly regular stuff.

At the beginning of the eighteenth century, however, when the novel first began to take on modern form, the available traditions of character depiction in fiction, as in biography, asked very different questions. Earlier biographies, whether real or imagined, were far more concerned to view individuals as belonging to or representing a certain general type than to understand them in all their human uniqueness. Cotton Mather, that notorious divine of Puritan Boston, published his magisterial study of New England history, the *Magnalia Christi Americana,* barely seventeen years before the appearance of *Robinson Crusoe,* but the understanding of character that shapes the two are light years apart. For Mather, there were pious widows, godly ministers, careworn magistrates—individuals who made sense only as they embodied age-old types of character often on the model of Biblical originals. For Defoe, character meant the rich uniqueness of individuality, particular people doing particular things. The truth of character for Defoe was not fidelity to scriptural precedent but fidelity to individual experience.

Mather was not ignorant of such details about the lives of his subjects. Many of them he knew personally; the rest, he knew about through family, colleagues, associates. He simply did not believe—nor did the tradition in which he operated believe—that these details were relevant. For purposes of biography, of character sketch, they were beside the point. They did not fall into the category of what was meant by biography. They were no more to the point than we think a senator's preference in breakfast meats is to our analysis of his or her legislative record. Then as now, such implicit categories define not only *what* we think but *how* we think.

These issues may seem far afield from those facing twentieth-century managers worried deeply about new competitive challenges. Not so—if, that is, we can distinguish the particular stuff we think about (notions of biography, constitutions, competitive challenges) from the way we do our thinking. Implicit categories, built out of the shreds and patches of shared experience, underlie it all.

By 1916 the top managers at Du Pont had begun to think about the long-term effects on their business of the huge expansion in plant, scope of operations, degree of vertical integration, and personnel brought about by World War I. Out of these considerations came a determination to enter several new lines of business, including the manufacture and sale of paints. Taken together these major efforts at diversification placed considerable strain on the company's administrative structure and, in fact, ultimately hastened Du Pont's move toward what we now think of as a decentralized mode of organization. At the time, however, what was clear was that many of these ventures did not show the financial results expected of them. The paint business, for example, lost nearly half a million dollars in 1919 on sales of just over $5 million. In the words of one internal study, "The more paint and varnish we sold, the more money we lost." Something was very much the matter. But what?[19]

Management opinion was divided. In the judgment of some within Du Pont, this lackluster performance was the predictable result of fatally overtaxing current administrative systems and principles. Any remedy less severe than rethinking the company's overall mode of organization would not have any lasting effect. In the judgment of others, the problems of the paint business were the temporary—and equally predictable—hiccups of the company's move into a new area. They were, literally, the price that had to be paid until managers became familiar with the right levels of raw materials to buy and inventory to carry, the right approaches to factory operation, the right structure of orders to encourage, and the right levels of selling expense. In other words, the problem at hand was, though certainly unpleasant, nothing to be alarmed about. It called only for a little patience, not a radical tinkering with the basic manner in which Du Pont functioned. The losses, after all, were par for the course in any start-up situation.

How, then, should the company respond to the troubles it was having with its paint business? More accurately, how should it define the nature of those troubles in the first place? Were they structural and serious, or were they likely to be ephemeral, the inevitable byproduct of a lack of experience? Half a century later, during the 1970s, the American automobile industry faced much the same kind of painful question. Was the beating it was taking from foreign imports a temporary blip on an otherwise healthy growth curve, the product of transient economic misfortunes linked directly to the policies of OPEC? Or was it the natural consequence of maturity in a domestic industry that had moved uncomfortably near the end of its life cycle? Or, perhaps, was it the result of specific management actions and systems that, whatever their past merits, no longer served the industry well?

For both Du Pont's paint business and the post-1973 domestic automobile industry, the facts of poor performance lay on the table for all to see. The issue, of course, was how to interpret them, how to know into which category of diagnosis they fell. As is so often the case with what managers, especially top managers, actually do, the task here was not so much to solve problems as to understand exactly what the problems were. In both cases, those who argued for interpreting current troubles as a painful but passing circumstance were in the wrong. We can see that clearly now about Du Pont; there are still arguments about Detroit. No firm rule can help managers make these discriminations with ease, but they can be made. At the least, the strain involved in maintaining that all is basically well, in pulling a tattered theory to cover new conditions, ought to give fair warning that bland assertions of the status quo are highly problematic.

Reducing the disorder of information into some sort of coherent problem is not to prepare the ground for management but to carry it out. Russell Ackoff, the well-known business scholar, puts it more simply: "Managers do not solve problems: they manage messes."[20]

Do Categories Soften?

We manage messes, in Ackoff's sense, by imposing a definition, a principle of order, on otherwise scattered bits and pieces of evidence. We look and look at everything strewn about the table top until something clicks, and the pattern in it all becomes clear. Much as, after a long bout of staring, we are suddenly able to "see" the point of an optical illusion, so after some process of mental sorting we are able, often without warning, to tell what the missing letters in the crossword puzzle are or what the figure in the carpet is. We finally see the pattern. This sort of pattern recognition makes clearer vision possible by establishing a principle of contrast. It may be well nigh impossible to see a white sheet of paper against an unbroken surface of white snow, but a dark swatch of material will show up immediately. In experiments with vision as in all areas of human activity, there are points at which one thing stops and another begins, and it is the fact of these boundaries that makes the character of each individual thing intelligible.

When does a chair stop being a chair and become a stool? How large a piece of pottery must we knock out of a ceramic vase before the object stops being a vase with a hole in it and becomes just a pottery shard? Is a table with one leg gone still a table? With two legs gone? With four? Most of the time our notions of most things, tangible or not, swim loosely in the midst of the comfortable spectrum of possible forms we allow each kind of thing to take. We can look at a wild variety of tables and never be troubled with doubt about the type of object at which we are looking. Push far enough, however, push too near the fuzzy boundary of our sense of what constitutes a table, and a given object may well confuse us. That confusion, which we have all felt at one time or another, is at base a puzzlement over categories, over proper definitions. Day to day, we assume boundaries are firm; every now and then they prove to be anything but.

Ought a person's appearance and personal history be part of a biographical sketch? Well, it depends. Was Du Pont's paint business in serious trouble? Did the loss of domestic auto sales in the mid-1970s mean a lasting change in how the automobile industry competes? Well, it is impossible to tell until we know *how* to look at the myriad of detail in front of us—that is, until we know how to manage, to clean up, the mess of fact.

What guides our knowing in such instances is our implicit sense of where the boundaries fall, where a healthy business with problems leaves off and a deeply troubled business begins. But these boundaries, remember, as well as the categories they define, are every bit as much a convention, a thing "built," as is our notion of an hour or a universally accessible calendar. Like other artifices, they so lull us into forgetting their nature as a thing constructed that we, in turn, rarely think of the idiosyncratic facts we need to add back. In practice, managing

messes requires that we first simplify disorder by imposing some principle of categorization and then carefully
remain aware that our categories inevitably leave important things out.

We need categories, but we are not done when we
have them. Their use obligates us to a new level of effort:
sustained attention to the particular details that so easily
slip away from institutional memory. We need to remember that old 78 rpm recording sessions took place in
four-minute stretches, even as we master the systematic
character of the new 33 rpm technology. We need to
remember all the details of the paint business at Du Pont
so that we can deal fairly with the particular, not just the
generic, problems facing it.

Left to themselves, categories harden. Certainly, the
maps of reality that result are important to us. We cannot effectively do without them. But the hardening process also distorts our vision as it makes it possible for us
to get messes of new detail under some sort of control.
Unless institutional memory corrects that distortion, or
at least calls it to our attention, we are likely to be obliv-
ious to the fact that it even exists. So natural and matter-
of-fact do we take our hardened categories to be, that we
find it difficult to believe—without memory's prodding
support—that things could be otherwise.

Other ways of ordering things may seem, literally,
inconceivable—not just something with which we dis-
agree, but inconceivable. Yet categories are cultural
forms, the product of social experience, in the same way
that a certain style in architecture is or a preference for

neckties or a legal prohibition against the Sunday deliv-
ery of mail. They may seem like natural parts of the
world, the way an hour does, but they are human creations nonetheless. Just as it is hard for us to imagine a
time when hours had uneven lengths, or when observers
doubted that Du Pont's paint business was in real trouble, it is hard for us to imagine that other people in other
circumstances position the normal boundaries of their
world in different places than we do.

That's the bad news. The good news is that such an
awareness need not be lost forever. Even if all that is left
is convention so dried and compressed that it seems like
a hard and elemental fact, there are ways for memory to
add back at least some of what has been lost over the
years. Much as the addition of water can bring dehy-
drated food back to life—not exactly as it once was, to be
sure, but close enough—a dose of history, of detail remembered, can help restore our recognition of artifice.
Because we have not altogether lost our capacity for
wonder, an isolated fact or series of facts can still bring us
up short by showing us something new about something
we thought utterly familiar.

It is the "illusion of knowledge" that most gets in the
way of accurate knowledge—for the man with a pocket
watch no less than for a manager needing to decide
whether Du Pont's paint business is really in trouble.
Consider, in this context, one of the business decisions
that we all think we know something about. By the late
1870s, the Western Union Telegraph Company had the
chance to dominate the nascent telephone business, but

it signed a contract with the Bell interests that effectively confirmed the Bell group's control of the industry. In any roll of honor for dumb managerial choices, the Western Union settlement usually ranks at the very top. In hindsight it seems a preposterous mistake. Certainly, it was a costly mistake. But was it, in fact, an error, a hideous goof? Untutored hindsight says of course; at the time, however, it made perfect sense.

We can understand the sense it made only if we make the effort to reconstruct how things seemed to Western Union in 1879. By assigning its telephone rights and patents to National Bell, Western Union did what it was most concerned to do: make safe its control over the telegraph. The agreement saw to it that local telephone exchanges served a rather limited area (usually a circle of fifteen-mile radius as measured from each central office) and carried only voice messages—that is, "personal communication." All business messages that went by wire were to go by Western Union's telegraph. Moreover, for a period of seventeen years Bell was to pay a 20 percent royalty on the rental income from all leased telephones. Thus, Bell would have to itself all the risk and expense of trying to make a business out of a commercially unproved technology, and Western Union, freed of a potential competitor, would take a nice cut off the top.

George David Smith, a historian who has studied this 1879 agreement, views the contract as

Western Union's way of assigning to the Bell Company the problems of managing the local loop, voice-grade communica-

tions systems attached to Western Union's nationwide telegraph network. With the market separated into local and
long-distance parts, Western Union stood to benefit in the
following way. As a captive feeder, Bell's business would en-
hance Western Union's telegraph traffic and revenues. Western Union, moreover, was freed from financing and managing
the relatively capital-intensive and technically complex telephone exchange operations.[21]

In the environment of post–Civil War America, who
could have known that the relations between the telephone and telegraph would not work out as Western
Union thought they would? It was, at the time, a reasonable guess—more than that, an excellent guess. It
simply turned out to be wrong. Knowing what the available facts were saves the decision from easy stereotype
and gives it back to us as what it was: a deliberate,
thoughtful attempt to deal with very real current problems and fears. By putting back the idiosyncratic historical detail, we can see much more accurately how it was
and what it meant. Our simple categories of retrospec-
tive judgment turn out not to be so simple after all.

Categories seem natural, for the most part, because
we are used to them. It could be otherwise. For instance, in the nonexistent Chinese encyclopedia imagined by the Argentine writer Jorge Luis Borges, all
animals must fall into one of the following categories:

(a) belonging to the Emperor, (b) embalmed, (c) tame, (d)
sucking pigs, (e) sirens, (f) fabulous, (g) stray dogs, (h) included
in the present classification, (i) frenzied, (j) innumerable, (k)

drawn with a very fine camelhair brush, (l) *et cetera*, (m) having just broken the water pitcher, (n) that from a long way off look like flies.

What matters about this lovely scheme of classification, as several commentators have noted, is that it literally boggles the mind. We cannot comfortably think it or think through it. There are, it turns out, some categories that cannot be thought or thought effectively. No conglomerate can be organized into divisions for food, beverages, and running errands.

According to the historian Robert Darnton, a classification scheme like that of Borges,

> by bringing us up short against an inconceivable set of categories . . . exposes the arbitrariness of the way we sort things out. . . . When confronted with an alien way of organizing experience, however, we sense the frailty of our own categories, and everything threatens to come undone. Things hold together only because they can be slotted into a classificatory scheme that remains unquestioned. We classify a Pekinese and a Great Dane together as dogs without hesitating, even though the Pekinese might seem to have more in common with a cat and the Great Dane with a pony. If we stopped to reflect on definitions of "dogness" or on other such categories for sorting out life, we could never get on with the business of living.[22]

Yet we act on implicit definitions of dogness—or, for that matter, of business success and failure—every day. All people do. We would feel utterly naked without them. More than that, we would feel powerless without them,

for the act of imposing or reaffirming a classificatory
scheme is an act of power. It establishes our notion of
what can exist in our world, what lies outside our notice,
even what makes our flesh crawl. We do not and cannot
see things that are not properly categorized. As Darnton
says, "A misshelved book may disappear forever." Some
things fall between the cracks—like the value of an
anaerobic adhesive at GE.

Indeed, the most dramatic example of the shaping
influence these categories have on us is our reaction to
those objects or animals or events that, while perfectly
visible, simply do not fit. Darnton again:

> Monsters like the "elephant man" and the "wolf boy" horrify
> and fascinate us because they slip in between categories:
> "slimy" reptiles that swim in the sea and creep on the land,
> "nasty" rodents that live in houses yet remain outside the
> bounds of domestication. We insult someone by calling him a
> rat rather than a squirrel. . . . Yet squirrels are rodents, as
> dangerous and disease-ridden as rats. They seem less threat-
> ening because they belong unambiguously to the
> out-of-doors.[23]

It is the things "in between" that really give us trouble.
A married woman colleague tells of trying to check into
a hotel in Korea while on a consulting visit and running
directly into a paralyzing cultural assumption that married women do not travel alone. The quick-witted hotel
manager solved the problem by saying to her in full view
of the staff, "Welcome to our hotel, sir."

Similarly, Western Union managers in 1879 could not

see the larger implications of the telephone for their business, or for business in general, because they quite reasonably thought about this new technology as an adjunct to telegraphy and the industry structures to which it gave rise. A century later, executives in Detroit were slow to apprehend the nature of the Japanese import challenge because, in a sense, the Japanese producers really were rats—that is, their mode of competing, the kinds of things they tried hard to be good at, violated entrenched assumptions about what was involved in designing and building a car. What they were trying to do fell "in between." In a world view conditioned by annual model changes and cosmetic marketing sizzle, cutting inventory to the bone did not seem like an effective, let alone a sensible, way to think about running a major capital goods business. To every newly landed Toyota on an American pier, someone in Detroit was moved to say, sotto voce, "Welcome to our country, sir."

The thing to remember is that the mostly invisible atmosphere of convention and artifice in which we live and work sustains us at the same time that it conditions what and how we think. Without it, we would truly be at a loss, confused and abandoned in a featureless landscape with no bearings to follow and no map to guide us. But we get our sense of direction at a price. True, the "as if" maps by which we steer are maps we must have. There is no point in wishing them gone; we have to have them. Even so, they shape how we think and provide us with the things we think with: the relevant objects and categories and relations in the world we inhabit. As

Churchill said of architecture, first we shape our buildings and then our buildings shape us. The danger lies not in using these maps or in relying on these conventions but in forgetting what they are and what they leave out. Long usage hardens our categories by draining away our awareness of artifice. Institutional memory—historical detail—puts it back.

Turtles All the Way Down

There is an Indian story—at least I heard it as an Indian story—about an Englishman who, having been told that the world rested on a platform which rested on the back of an elephant which rested in turn on the back of a turtle, asked . . . what did the turtle rest on? Another turtle. And that turtle? "Ah, Sahib, after that it is turtles all the way down."

—CLIFFORD GEERTZ

B<small>Y RESTORING</small> lost detail, institutional memory can retard or even reverse for a time the inevitable hardening of categories. It is the best instrument there is for slowing down the rate at which an awareness of artifice leaches away. At least, it can be. All too often, however, memory itself falls victim to the disease for which it alone possesses the remedy. In institutional settings, memory does not persist or get transmitted in a vacuum. It achieves its force—and finds its expression—through the apparatus of tradition, that complex social process for placing current experience and arrangements in the context of all that has gone before and, by so doing, legiti-

61

mizing them. Through the operation of memory, tradition provides a much needed source of authority in the present. But at a cost. When filtered through tradition, memory too can be purged of those details that help sustain an awareness of artifice.

In Chapter I we saw that the world about us is largely a world of convention, from which the awareness of artifice has drained away. The course we chart for ourselves through that world is not—and cannot be—a road we build anew with entirely new materials. The tools we use, the very ground we dig, the experience in road-building on which we call for assistance—all these may seem fresh to our hand or mind but are, in fact, the many-layered residue of past builders like ourselves. Like it or not, we live in time, and the fleeting moment of our present is heavy with the weight of all that presses upon it. We may try to forget or ignore the jumbled strata of the landscape before us, but that only makes us more awkward travelers than we need to be.

In this second chapter we take a closer look at the ways in which we take possession, as individuals and as members of organizations, of our place in time. By our participation in and with tradition, we come to share an understanding of the world about us that has, for us, a commanding sense of rightness and fitness. Because tradition is both a mode of knowing and the content of what is known, it creates its own legitimacy and confers that legitimacy on everything it touches. It calls on memory, but memory of a limited and partial sort. If the faded name on the militia rolls belongs to a man who crossed the Delaware with Washington that cold winter night, we possess more than a neutral fact about him. He has our thanks, our allegiance, our respect. We know all we feel we need to know about him. But the force that generates such emotional legitimacy is no respecter of changes in circumstance. To survive through time, organizations must survive *in* time, must turn perennial and predictable human responses to long-term institutional ends. But once a company or a town or an army or a church brings on-line the full apparatus of social commitment, once it moves the lever of tradition to its "full on" position, there is no quick or easy way to turn the system off or adapt it to other uses. The oil supertanker under full power cannot stop on a dime or turn on a nickel. The silent juggernaut of tradition is no different.

When the nation's financial markets went on their long spree during the 1920s, it was a fairly simple matter to grab a headline to lambaste an especially lurid piece of shady dealing or fast footwork. Were your Peruvian bonds not worth the paper they were printed on? Well, there was raw material for at least one set of Congressional hearings. Did your utility empire collapse under the weight of its own watered stock? Well, the career prospects of several federal prosecutors suddenly brightened. Did your investment firm secretly pay off financial writers to chant the praises of the securities it was about to float? Well, it was finally time to pull back the curtain that hid what went on in your back office. But did you adapt to market realities and float more common stocks than bonds? Well, yawn, who cared? Who cared if managers and investors, who were trained to calculate the values and risks associated with real property, found themselves marketing and purchasing new financial instruments linked, instead, to a company's projected earning power?

Who indeed? Not a headline, not a hearing, not a smidgen of publicity. The fact that America's financial infrastructure had begun to convert to a medium that no one really understood or knew how to evaluate raised nary an eyebrow among the public. Among the experts there was some quiet gnashing of teeth. "We, here, and our customers," noted one member of the Investment Bankers Association, "are groping around to find out what our equities are worth. . . . There is no yardstick for us to go by." But this was virtually a lone voice, raised in private.[24]

To most celebrants at the great financial barbecue, it seemed perfectly reasonable that people would continue to buy and sell as they had always bought and sold. Smart folks knew how to make money in the market; foolish amateurs lost their shirts. Nothing new in that. Smart folks knew what things were worth, knew how to read between the lines, knew how to pick out the important facts amid the florid legalese of financial offerings. The best of them had grown up in the business, had cut their eyeteeth on it. They were members in good standing of a pretty unforgiving fraternity, and the mere fact they were still in business meant they knew what they were doing. The trouble was, of course, that what they knew bore little relation to what they now had to

know. Their painfully acquired traditions of interpretation, analysis, and gut feel—no less than the confidence
to which these traditions gave rise—misled them. To
members of the fraternity, it seemed as if their remembered way of reading the value of securities held all the
answers.

Before we prove too free with our criticism of this rote
allegiance to outdated traditions, we ought spend a moment in front of the mirror. Just think, for example, of
the numbers we regularly treat as proxies for significant
economic realities. Our plants and factories still rely on
cost accounting systems that made sense when direct
labor accounted for the lion's share of total manufacturing costs, not for the 10 or 12 percent of those costs it
does today. And we still make projections based on the
government's leading economic indicators, the compo-
nents of which no longer tell a convincing tale about the
movements of the economy.

Growth in the supply of money—to cite but one obvious delinquent—does not mean an upturn in business
performance if the money is mostly being used to pay for
imports. Nor, for that matter, do many of the government's fabled "seasonal adjustments" capture the reality
they appear to capture. When the pattern of an industry's
sales or model introductions changes, imputing adjustments on the basis of older arrangements is just another
form of building castles in Spain. Say, there is a lovely
bridge in New York that you might like to buy.

Now, we all know this. No self-respecting manager
would pledge life savings and family as collateral for the

pristine accuracy of these numbers. Anyone who has ever spent time with market or economic forecasts knows perfectly well the amount of sodium chloride with which to season them. At the same time, however, we still find the habit of instinctive reliance hard to break. The numbers do, after all, have an appealing solidity—what Whitehead called, remember, a "misplaced concreteness"—and we do need to have some numbers to work with. Even though we know better, even though we are reasonably conscious of the difficulties involved, we still find much that is seductive in our traditional ways of thinking about things.

In this we are no better or worse than the bond brokers of the 1920s, who suddenly found themselves at sea on a flood of common stock.

Like the maps by which we steer, then, tradition is something we cannot do without at the same time that it has side-effects powerful enough to do us in. We have to be alert—and careful. This is no mean task.

As the discussion of categories and conventions in Chapter I tried to show, the normal circumstances of our lives invariably work to shield us from such moments of disorientation. The "built" character of our ideas and customs and beliefs and arrangements usually hides behind a screen of forgetfulness. Over time, as the awareness of artifice drains away, we learn not to look upon our understanding of, say, what an hour is as the product of Greek, Egyptian, and Babylonian science. We learn, instead, to think of it as a hard, plain nugget of fact. Pull the screen back, however, and put back the lost detail, and the whole dizzying vista of shreds and patches out of which that understanding has been slowly constructed once more comes into view.

So it is with the societies in which we live and the organizations in which we work. Like it or not, know it or not, we always stand in the midst of an apparently endless hallway—an expanse measured not in space but in time. The true extent of this corridor in time is regularly hidden from us. And for good reason. Were we to see it complete, were we to have the full picture-postcard view of all the turtles on which other turtles rested, we would likely have an attack of what polite folk in an earlier age called the vapors. Seen whole, the panorama is too much to take. We let the screen fall comfortably into place because we would otherwise have too much to remember.

For the most part, then, we operate by choice and necessity with a swaddled view of things. Salient facts remain conveniently out of sight. The picture made possible by their absence takes on an aura of sanctioned legitimacy that, in turn, makes the picture infinitely harder to question or dislodge. It is difficult enough to remember the artifice in our notion of an hour. When the full weight of how an organization remembers helps screen the fact of artifice, the task of recovering it is well nigh impossible.

By the late 1920s, for example, Alcoa had some thirty-two operations underway in countries other than the United States. In 1928 a variety of considerations, including antitrust considerations, led management to retrench and pull back from its aggressive postwar thrust into international activities, which were first transferred to a Canadian subsidiary and then severed from Alcoa proper when the subsidiary was spun off. Arthur Vining Davis, then the company's chairman, had doubts about Alcoa's ability to run matters well both home and abroad at the same time. The proliferation of tariff barriers in foreign markets added fuel to his concerns. To be fair, he also wanted to create a suitable top-level position for his brother, who became president of the Canadian firm. Good or bad, there were specific reasons for what Davis chose to do in 1928, and those reasons pointed to a reversal of the company's earlier movements into international operations.

Thirty years later, all the company remembered was that it was a domestic firm with a domestic orientation. Why this was the case had long been forgotten. That it was—even that it should be—the case was a simple fact, a nugget of corporate truth too obvious to be debated. Looking back on that period of untroubled certainty from a vantage point in the mid-1980s, a later chairman of Alcoa, Charles W. Parry, saw matters differently. According to Parry,

> The spin-off of our foreign activities in 1928, for reasons peculiar to that time, interrupted Alcoa's international development. It was an attitude about this event in our history, and not anything inherent in the nature of our abilities, our technology, or our markets that subsequently kept us isolated in the U.S. market for so many years.
>
> Even though opportunities were ripe much earlier, it wasn't

until the 1960s that we again ventured forth, in earnest, into the international arena. World War II demands for aluminum and the outstanding growth in consumption during the post-war years combined to reinforce what had become Alcoa's strong domestic mindset. It was a mindset that long outlasted the context of its creation.[25]

Mind-sets and Contexts

Outlasting the contexts of their creation is something, that mind-sets have a nasty habit of doing. Just as the "built" character of conventions becomes less visible over time, so too do the contexts of important decisions and actions—and mind-sets. We all remember, sort of, that Washington crossed the Delaware. Some of us may even recall the date. But few of us, indeed, save the history student or the military buff, can reconstruct in detail the full range of considerations that prompted him to act as he did when he did. The U.S. Constitution created a two-house legislature at the federal level. We know that it did. Those of us with a taste for colorful rhetoric and adept logrolling may have even watched the two houses in action. Virtually any schoolchild, certainly any one old enough to recognize concepts like influence peddling or cost-plus contracts, can name the two houses of the legislative branch. But who among us remembers the nice distinctions of political argument that led to this two-house system in the first place or the precise litany of concerns that its delicate balance was intended to address?

Marc Antony was wrong. It is not so much that the

good men do often dies with them while the evil survives. It is, rather, that *what* men do—their choices, their actions, their deeds—finds a ready place in memory while the reasons, the intended significance, of their deeds quickly float away out of reach and beyond recall. Many a Pharaoh left us a tomb in the shape of a pyramid. We have all seen at least a picture of one, even if only on a dollar bill or a cigarette package. We know that they exist. But as for the view of things, the statement of belief or hope, those pyramids represented, well, such mysteries have long since mixed themselves with the desert sand out of which they came.

There was a time when a flag or banner with the stylized image of a rattlesnake expressed the fiercest patriotic hopes of overmatched but tough-minded colonists. Today, there are museums and galleries that display some of those original pennants. In suburban malls there are teenagers with that same design stenciled on their T-shirts. We know the image and may even recall the occasion, but how many of us can talk sensibly for five minutes about the issues that were uppermost in the minds of the generation that sewed those flags and carried them into battle?

Alcoa in the years after World War II was not unusual in the degree to which its communal memory embraced the fact but not the rationale of earlier choices. It was, after all, an emphatically domestic company—and quite a successful one at that and for that reason. Thirty years of industrial experience drove that lesson home, reenforced it, turned it into an article of faith. Thousands of people came to maturity in management swaddled in that lesson's rich cloth of implication and direction. Mentors taught it to their charges, and they in turn spread it among themselves. After a while, though, none of them could remember why it was that Arthur Vining Davis thought it best to retrench in 1928 or that it was Davis who, for a plateful of reasons that must have seemed good to him at the time, turned an internationally minded organization into one with strict domestic horizons in its thinking.

This loss of memory is not unusual. When the major American automobile companies fell under a stiff challenge from imports during the 1970s, many armchair pundits roundly lambasted them for being so unmindful of markets and producers abroad. Industry managers themselves largely took it for granted that their perennially domestic orientation had left them asleep at the switch. What few recalled was that, during the first several decades of the century, both Ford and GM were aggressive exporters of automobiles and actively remained so—until protectionist barriers forced them to stop. That's precisely the point: Few recalled. In the same fashion, today's ardent critics of Big Steel's head-in-the-sand approach to investing in dynamic new process technologies laugh off the thought that things ever were different. So do most defenders. Lost in the shuffle of cynicism are Andrew Carnegie's bold early forays into new technical areas.

It is fascinating to watch closely how a mind actually dockets a fact. If we are at all alike, which in this sense

I suppose we are, we attach handy labels to things before we file them away. Later, when the inevitable question comes—"Say, who was the actor who played so-and-so in the movie of the same name?"—we pull the appropriate little bundle from memory and slyly respond that it was X, of course, adding one salient bit of gossip about his well-reported fling with what's-her-name. Chances are that that tidbit of gossip is all that we can possibly dredge up about that actor of glorious memory. After that, our well runs dry. Nothing left. For us, that actor will forever be the man of the fling and the starring turn as so-and-so. He may have translated the Bible into Coptic or swum the Dardanelles backward or amused his evenings (all, of course, save that special fortnight with what's-her-name) distributing food to the needy. But for us he wears, and will always wear, a simpler label.

A flag, a pyramid, a movie, a corporate mind-set— these are things that can and do easily outlast the special cluster of ideas, concerns, intentions, judgments, hopes, and fears in the midst of which they were first created. When the times and circumstances that made them pass away, they blithely note the event and return to the work of their own dogged perseverance. Again, as any manager knows who has ever wrestled with a bureaucracy that has long forgotten its original purpose and has become a grand master of self-preservation, both structures and mind-sets regularly outlive their proper contexts and so find themselves attached to all sorts of strange bedfellows over the years. The long arm of the past picks some rather strange pockets.

This is not an insignificant point. Not only do we forget easily enough; we are largely immune to evidence that we have indeed forgotten. The lack of fit between, say, a particular mind-set and a new cluster of circumstances—evidence that ought to set off warning bells—tends not to bother us because we recollect so little about the original cluster. Worse, we tend to read the linkage of mind-set and context as an arrangement that carries with it its own justification. If we think of the two together, they must belong together. What exists is right.

When the man in the corner has on a horizontally striped tie, a vertically striped shirt, a loud plaid jacket, and plaid trousers in still a different pattern, we note quickly that something here is not quite right. We want to know why the spectacle in front of us is the way it is. We see it as something requiring explanation.

When, however, Alcoa or GM or Ford perks right along for years doing a profitable domestic business, we have no corresponding impulse to say, Wait a minute, folks, something is wrong here, something that needs explanation. The fact of a mismatch between current environment and current mind-set is not always obvious and will not always draw attention to itself in public. The problem, if there is a problem, does not announce itself to us as such in terms we cannot ignore or overlook. Our friend in stripes and plaid excites a felt need for interpretation that a booming aluminum or automobile business simply does not.

The fact of mismatch may be there every bit as strongly, but we tend to miss it because we do not have before our

minds (or our mind's eye) all the pieces of the puzzle.
Were the calculations of Arthur Vining Davis in 1928 as
readily and inescapably visible to us in the present as a
pair of impossibly garish trousers is, we would be much
better able to say how well certain things went together.
Unlike the costume of our friend with the happy taste in
tailors, the considerations that Davis had in mind are not
readily visible, do not call attention to themselves, and
so do not excite a need for interpretation.

A Common Law for
Organization

Part of the difficulty with our swaddling, then, is that we
have a hard time knowing when it no longer fits. More
than that, we are predisposed to believe that it does fit,
no matter how extreme the "it" may be. With arrangements of whatever sort, especially if they are of long
duration, our reaction is likely to be to put the burden of
proof on those who would argue that something is rotten
in the state of Denmark. Left to our own devices, we
tacitly assume the operation of a kind of common law in
such things: What exists in the present is the distilled
product of long experience, examination, and challenge
and is, therefore, probably the right way for things to be.
If something were grossly wrong with those arrangements, they would never have survived intact as long as
they have. The mere fact that they exist is compelling
evidence that what exists is right.

Phrased so baldly, this common law impulse may seem

silly or innocuous, but it is neither. We have, for the
most part, internalized this common law traditionalism
in our judgment of things, an expectation that the way
things are carries with it a powerful aura of legitimacy.
What underlies our assumption is tradition.

In practice, tradition offers a way of knowing that in-
timately and inextricably connects what is known with a
deep sense of its appropriateness, its rightness or fitness
for use. It is the anchor about which a society or an
organization swings on a chain of varying length, nosing
at one or another distance into different winds and different directions but always linked to a firm point of
reference that tethers such explorations within bounds.
Certainly, from time to time that anchor may drag or the
chain snap, but as a rule, we experience the fact of con-
nectedness as a guarantee of safe harbor. For years, remember, Alcoa rode happily as a domestic-minded
operation and quickly got out of the habit of asking why
its horizons were what they are.

Thus, the way we remember things, combined with
the way that tradition gives a kind of common law justification to present arrangements, works to blind us to
the process of mind-sets or actions or decisions becoming severed from their original contexts. We tend not to
see it happening and, faced with the result, tend not to
see that it has happened. As a practical matter, we give
credence to what lies before us and respond eagerly to
its mechanisms of self-justification. We forget that it,
too, is a "built" thing in much the same way that our
notion of an hour is. And when our awareness of such

tradition-borne artifice drains away, as it inevitably does, only history—institutional memory—can put it back. When it is time to unwrap the swaddling, it is historical understanding that provides the firmest grip on the tightly wound cloth.

There are often hidden structural weaknesses in the linkage between a mind-set and context that only memory can make visible. No matter how strong that connection may look from a distance, no matter how eagerly tradition bids us to trust it, it may be deeply flawed. Events may never put it to the test, and so it may serve passably well. But if great stress is ever brought to bear, for whatever reason, any inherent falseness in the linkage will make itself felt in troublesome and often unpredictable ways. When we credit knee-jerk attacks on bigness in business, we forget that a much-revered antitrust policy, which was framed by the circumstances of America in 1890, speaks with only limited relevance to the competitive realities of today's global industries.

Yes, such lack of fit becomes visible in the light of memory. But there is more. Mind-sets are not neutral things, fitting easily or poorly into their environments. They structure both how people come to think and act and, more than that, what acceptable notions of thought and action are. Like the first layer of cannonballs on a courthouse lawn, they define the patterns and possibilities open to the second layer and the third. By reconstructing how that first layer was set down, we can better understand not only the weak points in current arrangements legitimized by tradition but also the range of possible alternatives.

Do not, however, underestimate the staying power of tradition. When manufacturers began to put digital alarm clocks in aircraft cockpits, their much greater precision (as compared with the older analog clocks) proved of considerable value. At the same time, however, because these digital clocks operated on a twenty-four-, not a twelve-, hour cycle, it became easy for pilots who were used to twelve-hour cycles to set the alarm correctly for the hour they wanted but to confuse A.M. settings with P.M. settings. In the words of one observer, pilots began to make an entirely new kind of blunder: "the precise twelve-hour error."[26]

When American farmers first began to cultivate large corn fields with horse-drawn plows, they soon adopted the practice of planting the rows of corn a fixed number of inches apart in order to accommodate the width of the plow and its rigging. Years later, when gasoline-driven plows replaced the older models, farmers did not change the distance between their corn rows. Not at all. Plow manufacturers built their machines to operate within these fixed limits.

Today, as manufacturers scramble to update their plants and factories by introducing automated equipment like robots and so-called FMS (flexible manufacturing system) technology, they commonly apply their expensive new capabilities as a means for replacing direct labor. They take human workers off the production line and put these microprocessor-based machines in their place. The intent, of course, is to save labor costs and cut the amount of variation that human labor adds to any process. What most of these manufacturers are actually doing, however, is injecting sophisticated technology into a process designed for people, not redesigning the process to accommodate what the technology can do.

The point is simple: the implicit logic and design of arrangements well-suited to one kind of environment can easily—and comfortably—find themselves at work in other environments where the fit is much less appropriate. Earlier decisions, actions, and views of the world have a sneaky way of making themselves at home in later circumstances, where they do not entirely belong—and, of course, an equally sneaky way of doing so without anyone noticing that the fit is no longer appropriate.

If the early settlers of seventeenth century Massachusetts towns laid out their house plots and common lands in pretty much the same way that their ancestors had laid out towns and villages in England, it was not because they said to themselves, Let's make Codfish Center into a spitting image of old Crackerjack-upon-Gewgaw. Nor was it because they saw an immediate parallel between the situation in Crackerjack, where for centuries there had been no land to spare, and Codfish, which was a frontier outpost surrounded by great stretches entirely empty of settlement. The good people of Codfish did what they did—and as they did—because they had long since internalized how to lay out a town. Clustering individual house plots around an area of com-

mon land was, purely and simply, the way things were
done.

Were we able to hex the calendar and plop ourselves
down in the midst of the Codfish elders in order to tell
them there were other ways to proceed, they would no
doubt look at us as if we had come from another, quite
alien world—which, in fact, would be exactly the case.
Should push come to shove, the ministers and magistrates of Codfish would likely consider our thoughts on
locating vacation homes (along golf course fairways) in
the same light they would a recommendation to lace up
their shoes and button their collars—which, in fact, was
the exact reverse of what they maintained all good people should do. Before we laugh too hard at the traditions
of devout Codfishery, however, we ought to remember
that their shoes stayed on and their collars stayed up and
their towns stayed vital much longer than any newfan-
gled resort community of our acquaintance.

Not only do mind-sets become severed from their
original contexts and then infect, through tradition, the
contexts to which they later become attached. Circumstances often prompt the construction of mind-sets that
seem venerable but that never really existed before. (See,
for example, the discussion of Scottish Highland dress in
Chapter IV). Just as the lady down the block may coat
her new table with an antique stain in order to make it
look instantly old or buy a pair of prewashed jeans in
order instantly to enjoy the pleasure of sustained wear,
there are many situations that enjoy the aura or the appearance of immediate longevity. Think how rapidly a

consumer brand, once it wins acceptance, feels to its loyal customers as if it had been there forever.

In the great nineteenth century controversy over the age of the world, stimulated by the arguments of Darwin and evolutionary science, the men of religion who relied on the strict biblical reasoning of Bishop Ussher to claim that the world had been created in 4004 B.C. had to explain one way or another the existence of fossils. Their ingenious solution was to assert that yes, indeed, the world was created in 4004 B.C.—but that it was created with all the age-old fossils already in it.

So, too, with the operation of certain mind-sets and views of the world. As, for example, when American reformers during the Jacksonian era turned their attention to the problem of punishing and correcting criminal behavior, they gradually hit upon a new model for what prisons or penitentiaries should be: "physically imposing and highly regimented settings," as one historian describes them, "in which [convicts moved] in lockstep from bare and solitary cells to workshops, clothed in common dress, and forced into standard routines. . . ." Why this approach, so different from the local and relatively informal jails of the past? The reformers, governed by a wish to restore discipline and manners to a people they saw as corrupted and led astray by the social disorders of nineteenth-century life, very much wanted to build an institutional mechanism that was capable of reproducing the social order they believed had existed in earlier times.

The hope and intention, then, were to re-create a

world "in which men knew their place." The result of their efforts, however, was ironic indeed:

> Here sentimentality took over, and critics in the Jacksonian period often assumed that their forefathers had lived together without social strain, in secure, placid, stable, and cohesive communities. In fact, the designers of the penitentiary set out to re-create these conditions. But the results, it is not surprising to discover, were startlingly different from anything that the colonial period had known. A conscious effort to instill discipline through an institutional routine led to a work pattern, a rationalization of movement, a precise organization of time, a general uniformity. Hence, for all the reformers' nostalgia, the reality of the penitentiary was much closer to the values of the nineteenth than the eighteenth century.[27]

Not only did the reformers' efforts have the opposite result of the one intended; they also grew out of a set of assumptions about the nature of eighteenth century life that had no basis save in the reformers' own fond imaginations. Yet these reformers were quite certain they were on the right track—both in terms of what to do and in terms of what it was they were trying to recapture. In their minds, the fact of a cohesive social order during the colonial period was as real and self-evident and valuable as a model for later action as the fact of the Revolution itself.

This is not uncommon. Past mind-sets often linger on and condition responses to quite different sets of circumstance. When such mind-sets did not actually exist in the past, we sometimes take the additional step of creating them out of whole cloth and treating them as if they had been there all along. If our swaddling is not dense or tight enough, we are not beyond creating more of it and packing it more firmly about us. It is no accident that early efforts to design robots focused on the attempt to re-create human skills—but skills of a precision unmatched by any flesh-and-blood worker. Or that electronic typesetting equipment spaces words on the page with such rigorous exactitude that the eye finds their placement objectionable.

Whatever the arena, then, tradition operates in funny ways; and as we shall see in a moment, the funniness of its operation is not likely to change. No earnest plea for a different approach to penal reform would have convinced these Jacksonian thinkers that their larger goals were inappropriate, let alone beyond reach. No fragment of an early hominid from Olduvai Gorge would have pushed the researches of Bishop Ussher off their firm basis in strict biblical chronology. No vague recollection of past international activities would have been enough to shake Alcoa out of its domestic orientation. New-style prisons, biblical chronology, and competitive strategy—like the distance between rows of corn in an Iowa field—were as they were because that was the way people felt they ought to be. And where does the "ought" come from? What is the source of the invisible magnetic field that pulls the needle of practice always toward north? For that matter, whence derives the conviction that north is, after all, where we want to go? In a word, tradition.

Things Passed On

Why this ability to enlist loyalty and confer legitimacy?
Why the unique staying power of tradition? Precisely
because it is not something built from scratch but, rather,
something passed on, something transmitted through the
most venerable of social forms and practices. Remember
our friends in Codfish Center. What held their fragile
new settlement together and kept them from spinning
off into all sorts of eccentric courses? What gave conviction to their dry mutual assertions of how things ought to
be done? Surely not the bald fact that a bailiff might say
thus-and-such was the law. People may be humbled by
force or circumstance into obeying laws of which they do
not approve, but no group's ardent embrace of a way of
life has ever grown out of anything other than its own
volition. The powers that be may keep us from building
a house just where we want to, but we will not applaud
that prohibition unless it squares with our own deep
sense of how things should be. The elders of Codfish did
not set out into the wilderness armed only with a barren
checklist of do's and don'ts. Nothing of the sort. Instead,
they carried inside themselves a living vision of how
people went about the kind of life they hoped to lead.
Their evidence and argument were of a piece: Traditions
told them what was necessary and made them feel that
what was necessary was right.

A youngster learning how to play baseball may try to
ape the batting stance of a favorite major leaguer, but

such imitation at the plate will last only as long as the stance comes to feel right and natural in itself. In time it may become dysfunctional, a bad habit hard to break, but for the nonce it is a vital means of connection with the larger world in which that youngster desperately wishes to participate. The stylized behavior, the formulaic response—these are not the rote answers to an alien catechism. They are, instead, the outward signs of a critically important dialogue that that youngster is trying to carry on with the environment around him or her. The stance itself is not something to be learned the way a schoolbook lesson is learned, nor does it lend itself to factual testing. (Quick, don't check your book; tell us whether the left hand should be a bit higher and the shoulders more square to the plate.) It is not the stuff of a quiz, not something to be memorized like the date of a famous military invasion. It is something to be passed on like a flair for giving excellent holiday parties—or a knack for hitting.

Tradition can, as we have seen, help sustain an attachment to a given mind-set long after the context in which it originated and to which it responded has disappeared or undergone substantial change. When the hold of tradition is strong enough to block out awareness of the disappearance of context, we find ourselves in the position of a certain she-cat of Mark Twain's acquaintance that sat down on a hot stove lid. "She will never sit down on a hot stove-lid again, and that is well," Twain tells, "but also she will never sit down on a cold one any more." That is, we may find ourselves paying allegiance to a misleading or partial or limited construction of events while feeling that we are acting on the best universal wisdom available. The apparatus of traditional commitment is not readily able to distinguish the true prophet from the imposter.

Remember, too, that tradition works its effects less by the authority of specific remembered facts than by folk wisdom—the cumulative self-legitimization of what has lasted into the present. We underestimate the mental and emotional force of such common law precedent at our peril. Robert Frost's "Mending Wall" is the reminder of a famous bit of country wisdom: "Good fences make good neighbors." In the poem Frost wonders why this should be so and, further, if it should be so in every case. The man who cites the line to Frost believes it implicitly, having learned it from his father years back. It is traditional knowledge of the purest sort and has all the practical force of unquestioned religious belief. From Frost, the countryman's aphorism elicits not agreement but a recognition that the man "will not go behind his father's saying." In the rural universe of the poem, however, as in the executive suite at Alcoa or Ford or GM, the "father's saying" is more than enough to compel willing assent.

These are powerful forces we are talking about, often invisible in their operation but compelling in their effects. And they draw, as we have seen, on equally compelling in-built modes of response. Tradition is a great engine, and we are wired for it—although we do not usually understand how that engine runs, how its current moves us, or how the whole mechanism of communal energy can go wrong.

"In the early days of the last war," reports the historian of technology Elting Morison in a well-known story,

> when armaments of all kinds were in short supply, the British . . . made use of venerable field pieces that had come down to them from previous generations. The honorable past of this light artillery stretched back, in fact, to the Boer War. In the days of uncertainty after the fall of France, these guns, hitched to trucks, served as useful mobile units in the coast defense. But it was felt that the rapidity of fire could be increased. A time-motion expert was, therefore, called in to suggest ways to simplify the firing procedures. He watched one of the gun crews of five men at practice in the field for some time. Puzzled by certain aspects of the procedures, he took some slow-motion pictures of the soldiers performing the loading, aiming, and firing routines.
>
> When he ran these pictures over once or twice, he noticed something that appeared odd to him. A moment before the firing, two members of the gun crew ceased all activity and came to attention for a three-second interval extending throughout the discharge of the gun. He summoned an old colonel of artillery, showed him the pictures, and pointed out this strange behavior. What, he asked the colonel, did it mean. The colonel, too, was puzzled. He asked to see the pictures again. "Ah," he said when the performance was over, "I have it. They are holding the horses."[28]

We had, therefore, best understand a bit more than we do how tradition works because we, too, spend so much time holding the horses.

II

Now, what is so awful, the equine fancier may wonder, about stumbling through the day with traditional—and invisible—horses in tow? Were those artillery gunners hurting anyone by snapping rigidly to attention? Certainly, their behavior does not represent the height of military efficiency, but is its charming eccentricity anything to worry about? After all, in the military, as in many other structured areas of life, it is the fact of tightly disciplined behavior—response that can be counted on in definable sets of circumstances—that is of the greatest importance.

In fact, quite a lot. Our dress-parade soldiers and, more important, their beribboned officers know precisely what they are doing and why. Landed at night in the midst of a hostile firefight, they would not form up in marching ranks and wait for the flag bearers to pull on their white gloves. There is no confounding of parade ground with battleground, no confusion of marching order with the order of battle. The traditions of the drill have their uses in building discipline and esprit de corps. That is why conscious and intentional use is made of them. For the artillery unit Morison describes, however, there is no such express purpose underlying their rote behavior, no such clarity of context and response. There is only the unthinking, virtually instinctive flash of traditional action. Worse, there is no real understanding that that is what is taking place.

The Joys of Horse Holding

Much of the horse holding in organizations, large and small, is of this latter type. Not only does such knee-jerk observance of tradition often lack practical value; it seems perfectly natural, right, and fitting and, as a result, lends an air of ease to the whole performance. We have seen how tradition works silently to create its own legitimacy in the minds of those who participate in it. What we must also recognize is that the legitimacy so created works, in turn, to smooth over present concerns and reduce the sense of threat or challenge presented by novel circumstances. It makes us comfortable and complacent.

In the South Pacific, anthropologists tell us, there are island societies that have built elaborate traditions around some of the junk left behind by American servicemen during World War II. These so-called "cargo cults" take as their central object the veneration of an abandoned Coke bottle or a tin of processed meat. By weaving that tin or bottle into an elaborate system of traditional behavior, these societies sustain themselves and cherish the hope that the men who left the objects behind will one day return. In practice, the mechanics of the cult bring a feeling of peace and well-being to those who share in it, a deep sense that they have done all they can possibly do to address the main issues of their lives. Just as the obsessive personality who must step on every crack in the sidewalk feels a great wash of ease when each crack is ritually attended to, so these island peoples enjoy the ease that carrying on their traditions affords them.

It is easy to laugh at this veneration of a Coke bottle, although there will be those in Atlanta who think such soft-drink genuflection a perfectly reasonable attitude. The truth of the matter, however, is that we are far more like these islanders than we care to admit. We, too, hold our horses because it feels good to hold them and because the idea of letting go makes us feel uncomfortable. More than a little comfort comes from effective swaddling in tradition. And in the face of chill winds or uncertain environments, we tend to pull the wrapping about us more tightly still.

This is not mere rhetoric. As much research has shown, when companies or industries whose products rest on a given technology fall under threat from products that have a different technological base, their usual response is to deny the appeal of the new approach and to try to do better what they are already doing. As my colleague Dick Foster notes, this pattern of reaction is so common that it has a name, the "sailing ship phenomenon," which refers to the course followed by builders of sailing cargo ships during the nineteenth century when steam-powered ships first began to make their presence felt. What the established builders did was not to explore the possibilities of steam but to experiment with a variety of improvements in sailing ship construction. Add another mast, they thought, then another and another. That will do the trick. Well, it did for a while, for there were improvements to be made. But there were limits to how far these incremental tinkerings could go, and the folks most devoted to tweaking the performance of the old technology did not notice they were about to sail into a harbor from which there was no exit.

Modern critics of management often point to the operation of this phenomenon in a wide range of industries. How few were the makers of fan engines for airplanes that made the transition to jet engines. How few the makers of vacuum tubes that made the transition to transistors—and of transistors that made the transition to integrated circuits and semiconductors. When automobile tire construction went from bias-ply to radial or from cloth belt to nylon belt to steel belt, where were the folks who had done well early on? Pick an industry or a product category, and the odds are that this pattern has shown itself there, too.[29]

At times, of course, the decision to stick to one's last can be an eminently sound managerial choice. As followers of the stock market have good reason to know, the wild conglomerate urge of the market's go-go years has not, in most cases, led to high levels of performance among the swollen, random creatures thus produced. Choosing to focus on a business one understands, choosing to pass up the momentary allure of headline-grabbing but implausible combinations—these are, to be sure, the stuff of responsible professionalism. Across the spectrum of industries, however, and deep in the vitals of most individual companies, the impulse to keep things pretty much as they are is less a reasoned choice than a reflexive grab for the swaddling. And even where managers correctly think of themselves as having stepped up to the tough decisions and made them on their merits, what goes on day-to-day throughout their companies rarely reflects the deliberate choices made at the top. Chances are, the fellow with his hand out in the office down the hall is not waiting to shake on a radical change in procedure. He is holding a horse.

We even know the horse's name. It is tradition. Consider for a moment the experience of one especially noteworthy stable, the electric utility industry. For nearly a century managers in that industry had seen, without fail, a steady improvement in technological performance, productivity, and the costs of generating each kilowatt-hour of electricity. During that same period, they had increasingly relied on the outside manufacturers of their equipment for the R&D necessary to keep the steady flow of improvements coming. They had also learned to expect an equally regular growth in demand for the electricity they produced. This was the world they knew, and they had come to know it so well that they had grown confident it was the only world possible. For each year's plan, all they had to do was add new numbers to last year's trend line. In the words of one student of the industry, its "managers . . . felt proud of their achievements and considered themselves socially responsible stewards of technological progress and improved standards of living." And they knew what to do to keep feeling proud: more of the same.[30]

We can now look back on this pride and confidence from the far side of a falloff in the rate of technical progress, of a disastrous experimentation with nuclear and large-scale fossil plants, of an upward swing in generation costs, and of a slowing down of growth in demand. What we see from our vantage point is not a happy picture of effective stewardship but a broken landscape of complacent assumptions. There was, to be sure, no way for utility industry managers to foresee just how the future would play out, no way to tell that virtually every point of reference in their world would get stood on its head. But neither was there any reason for them to assume so blindly that everything would continue just as it was. It is one thing not to be able to predict exactly what questions the future will throw in the face of current assumptions. It is quite another to take for granted that no such questions will be asked. And another still to read the first unwelcome answers in so untroubling a light.

When we ask, Why such blindness, why such narrowness of vision? we cannot responsibly mean, Why was their crystal ball so terribly cloudy? Everyone's is. With justice, however, we can ask why they never allowed or encouraged themselves to think that some real change was possible, that something in their accustomed universe might just give way.

To this later question, perhaps the truest response is to repeat Robert Frost's characterization of the rural fel-

low who thought that good fences make good neighbors,
always and ever. He would not, Frost tells us, "go behind his father's saying." The force of tradition—of a
saying oft-repeated in shared setting by a respected el-
der—held this man. So, too, did it hold a generation and
more of utility managers. It made them, like him, comfortable with inherited belief, so comfortable in fact none
of them ever thought to look beyond or behind it, never
felt the need to, never imagined it to be important. Truly
effective swaddling not only keeps us in place; it is so
much a given part of our world that we fail to notice how
tightly it packs us in or even, for that matter, that it is
there at all.

The Dilemma of Tradition

When a new corporate sponsor and an aging celebrity
decide to cook up yet another made-for-television golf
tournament, we can be sure they will call it the Holly-
wood Facelift Classic or something of the sort. That is,
they will reach by instinct or shrewd calculation for the
language of tradition in the hopes of fooling someone
into viewing their efforts as partaking in a kind of instant
heritage. No one gets fooled, of course, and the rank
newness of the event will quickly show through its "classic" trappings, just as the course at which it is held will
show the footprints of some recently departed devel-
oper. To every eye, the fact of artifice will be obvious. To
Frost's neighbor, however, as to the dyed-in-the-wool
utility manager, the fact of artifice is both invisible and

unthinkable. They see not the swaddling of tradition; they see, so they think, the way the world really is.

Here, finally, we come to the central dilemma that tradition poses for life in organizations. Think, again, of our rural fence mender and our complacent utility executive. We may criticize their breadth of vision and point to the real-world penalties they must pay for seeing things in so constrained a fashion. But we cannot deny the vitality, confidence, purpose, and direction that their inherited views confer upon them.

These days, as we hear endless injunctions to managers to build commitment and a sense of community among the people in their companies, we must admire— even if with a twinge of irony—the deeply internalized loyalty and the visceral allegiance that both fence mender and utility executive show to their organizations or their organized modes of life. We know by now something about the kind of force tradition has and about the degree to which we are "wired" for it and vulnerable to it. Here we see, at least in outward terms, what that force can do in practice, which turns out to be just the sort of thing we have been turning over heaven and earth to create in the ranks of workers and managers. We say we want what our fence mender has and has in abundance, yet we can readily appreciate the limitations of his manner of engagement with the world. What to do?

From the example of our instant golf classic, we know perfectly well that jerry-built, prefabricated traditions may look wonderful in press releases but fool no one and have no real power to excite deep loyalty or a lasting

sense of commitment. Those of us who grew up with the
great professional sports teams of a generation ago look
with jaundiced eye on the movable franchises and the
musical-chair athlete of today's late-night cable broad-
casts. The call on our emotion and attention is outwardly
the same, but we are not taken in by that. The world we
knew and cared about and believed in ended when the
Dodgers went west—except, of course, for that saving
remnant in Boston that goes by the name of the Celtics.

Good hype and publicity can, of course, gin up momentary excitement, but it is feverish and has no staying
power. In sports as in politics or religion or management, manipulation of public image goes only so far and
lasts only so long. For the abiding sense of community
and allegiance that we want, there is no substitute for
organic, long-standing tradition. The Catholic Church
has not endured as long as it has or continued to elicit
the loyalty that it does because those who are drawn to
it are drawn by false promises or meretricious posturing.
A lasting organizational presence cannot rest on the
clever manipulation of image or the sham of instant longevity. It develops only over time from the slow operation of genuine tradition—the real goods. If our fence-
mender thought his father had first learned about what
makes good neighbors a week before in the *Reader's
Digest*, we may reasonably assume that he would not
hold to that bit of paternal wisdom as ardently and un-
questioningly as he does.

Thus, for the kind of vital organizations we want, we
need to nurture and extend the reach and power of tra-

dition. But to deal openly and intelligently with the realities of changing circumstance, we need to fight off the hold tradition has on our vision of things. To build real commitment, we must have effective tradition. But to avoid holding the horses, we must expose the artifice through which tradition works. We can enlist deep loyalty only by allowing genuine tradition to flourish. But we can go behind our father's saying only by allowing ourselves to see that that saying is relative and contingent, a partial view of the world from which our awareness of artifice has drained away. For reasons of community, we must have tradition organic and whole. For reasons of judgment, we must know it to be a thing "built" or constructed. Again, what to do?

Left unresolved, this dilemma can have troubling consequences. In the years after World War II, for example, the makers of farm equipment had seriously to adjust their thinking to one of the great prewar advances in tractor design: the Ford-Ferguson tractor's three-point hitch with a hydraulic system that worked for both draft and position. Here is what happened at Deere:

> Deere's hitches could not be controlled hydraulically for draft, so several company factories began experimenting, each on its own. . . . The real push and tug was between the Waterloo Tractor Works and the Plow Works, longstanding rivals in the company. Before the advent of the tractor, the Plow Works had been center stage, the main actor—after all, was not the plow the most important bread-and-butter product? Pride, a sense of importance, was still a legacy there. Similarly, the Tractor Works saw itself in the same light—was not the tractor

now the real bread-and-butter product, dominating all others in dollar volume, in profit? Pride and a sense of importance were in abundance there, too.

An important step toward bridging the gap between the two touchy groups came in 1949 with the establishment of the tractor and implement committee, which had high-level representatives from both operating groups, as well as central staff people from the experimental and product planning groups (and was chaired by one of the latter). Still, rivalry and jealousy between the two operating entities persisted and now surfaced once again as each insisted it had the right to develop the definitive version of hitch. "After all, the hitch is at the end of our tractor," said Waterloo. "No, it's our implement that is to be positioned," said the Plow Works.

Each finally developed its own version, but neither would give ground.[31]

Sound familiar? Is there any follower of, say, recent discussions about the United States military's chain of command or procurement practices who does not recognize in this face-off between the Plow Works and the tractor group at Waterloo the same issues of intraorganizational rivalry that continue to plague our uniformed services? Is there any organization large enough to be internally subdivided that does not regularly confront such battles over turf, priority, position, and pride?

Now, we want such emotions and group loyalties to flourish. We want the makers of plows to think that the world turns on an axis of their own fabrication. We want the builders of tractors to view members of every other occupational group, even within the same company, as a slightly lower form of life. We want our naval officers and enlisted personnel to think that every mission truly worth doing is a mission they ought to man and control. And we want the same from our other services, too. We want fierce pride and commitment to be as natural to these folks as the air they breathe. We want them to think they can do anything, to be ready to reach for levels of accomplishment ostensibly beyond their most eager grasp. Odds are, we would look at the Plow Works manager who meekly turned over responsibility for hitch development to Waterloo as a softy, a quitter, a fellow we didn't really like having on our team.

At the same time, of course, we want our people to be able to see beyond their own noses and to keep things in perspective. We want them to understand that what is best for the whole organization might not be best for their own part in it. We want them, by instinct as well as training, to think dispassionately about larger goals and the common, not just the local, good. We want them to be sharp enough analytically to judge when they and their people really should be on the point and when that honor and responsibility should belong elsewhere. In short, we want them to be able—full of tradition as they are—to stand up and say, in effect, We can see right through the artifice of our own binding traditions, those things we hold closest and most dear, and agree that our hearts and heads are leading us in a wrong direction.

Put simply, we want the impossible. Our wish is to put the medicine of tradition to work in its strongest form without suffering any of its inevitable side-effects. Like the lady in the limerick who decided to ride the tiger, we forget how easy it is to wind up inside. At some level, we hope that our Plow Works manager is a true believer but filled with rampant inner doubt, a self-questioning zealot, a temperate idealogue. We hope to tap the deepest commitments of which he and his people are capable, but we would prefer to do so by turning them on and off like a spigot. It does not work that way.

At Deere, predictably, there were no easy compromises. Neither group backed off from its position. Even when the hitch designed by the Plow Works showed itself to be inferior, the fact that it was an adaptation of an earlier, venerable design reinforced the sentiment of those already determined to stand by it. With no treaty in sight,

> top management finally decided to hold a field contest between the two. In the ensuing match, the Waterloo version won hands down. The Plow Works remained unreconciled, predicting "disaster" if the Waterloo hitch was adopted. Only after a compromise was arranged—that the Plow Works could build 1,000 of its hitches, to be stockpiled until the disaster struck—was the conflict settled. . . . The Waterloo hitches turned out to work very well and soon were adopted for all the company machinery; the 1,000 stockpiled Plow Works hitches were scrapped.[32]

If we are honest, we must admit that the organizations we know best are positively littered with the debris of such compromises. That is, quite literally, the price we pay for having our people enmeshed in a vital, energizing tradition. Yes, it is messy, sloppy, and inefficient, but we would be reluctant to sacrifice the many benefits of tradition for a neater, more streamlined payment of lip service to organizational goals. We may lament the costs of tradition, but we are not willing to do without. Still, we may ask whether operating on this stockpiled middle ground is the best we can do.

III

The Language of the River

> Now when I mastered the language of this water and had
> come to know every trifling feature that bordered the great
> river as familiarly as I knew the letters of the alphabet, I had
> made a valuable acquisition. But I had lost something, too.
> I had lost something which could never be returned to me
> while I lived. All the grace, the beauty, the poetry had gone
> out of the majestic river!
>
> —MARK TWAIN

WHEN MODERN ARCHEOLOGISTS first discovered
the site of the ancient city of Troy, they found that it was
not one city but seven, each built on top of the ruins of
those that came before. To no one's surprise, the 1,000
hitches manufactured by the Deere Plow Works could
not be located anywhere in that immense layer cake of
civilization—not least because it would be centuries before the company got around to making them. In a sense,
though, they might as well have been there. At Troy, as
in the heartland of American agriculture, the very ground
we build on is rich with the debris of tradition.

Whatever the institutional setting, then, the past finds

a way to make itself felt in the present. At the least, it deeply conditions the categories through which our world gets built and understood. Equally important, the past gets mediated to the present in a self-legitimating fashion that fosters social cohesion and makes commitment possible. This is what we mean when we talk about tradition, that common law process for knowing who we are and what we do—and feeling comfortable about both. To the extent we lack a keen awareness of artifice, however, we are often blind to just how partial and limited our knowledge really is. And being blind, we are virtual prisoners of those limitations.

Such is the argument of the first two chapters. There is no use lamenting our vulnerability to tradition, to the "passed on" conventions of our world. Like it or not, we are wired that way. Moreover, being wired that way has its virtues. It is no small matter to want to be the best darn hitch builders that ever were. It does not follow, however, that such unavoidable circuits of response doom us to eternal prisoner status. There are things we can do—first, of course, reminding ourselves continually that the matter-of-fact universe through which we pick our way is every inch the long-term product of artifice. But we can do more. We can learn to pay attention to the way tradition works, the way it produces its effects. Understanding more about the "how" of tradition—the mechanisms by which it influences our judgment and action—is the task to which this chapter sets itself.

Indeed, for those of us whose organizational lives are spent in Troy, mired in the debris of level upon level of tradition, there is great value in learning exactly how being a Trojan affects the way we see the world. The fact that we stockpile unnecessary hitches is, by itself, merely curious. The fact that we usually do so without thinking—and that we accept a hitch-littered environment as perfectly natural—is something else again. Even if we wanted to, we could not purge our environment of all such remnants. Nor should we want to. Many of them are terribly important to us. But we ought not to ignore the mechanics by which they hold us.

As we have seen, what we possess through tradition has a deep influence on what we know and, more importantly, on how we think. Ask why our structure of national government was intended by its framers to provide a series of checks and balances, and even a high school student will recite the litany of colonial grievances against executive prerogative, Star Chamber excess, and legislative fiat. Ask, instead, why those grievances led to a form of government based on the principles of Newtonian mechanics, and the answer is likely to be an uncomfortable silence. The use of each branch of government to limit the power of the others is a fact we find easy to know and remember. The use of mechanics to define the relations of governmental structures is, by contrast, a way of thinking we find hard to recognize or keep in focus.

Why did that generation of late eighteenth-century political leaders think the way they did about the importance of balancing mechanical forces against each other? Why, for that matter, did a later generation of leaders—

the ones who flourished in the two decades before the Civil War—think in quite different terms of irreconcilable conflicts and unbreachable fissures in the body politic? After all, there had been serious rifts in the days of empire too.

Both generations of leaders saw powerful groups in the society whose interests were mutually incompatible. Both saw the threat of aggrandizement by established institutions. Both saw a real possibility that the political center might not hold. But why did one generation think in terms of mechanical balances and the other in terms of structural cracks and fissures? Yes, the political circumstances of 1850 were markedly different from those of 1780. But if that were all that had changed, why did not the generation of Calhoun and Webster simply turn their energies to the search for new principles of mechanical balance?

What these questions overlook is the fact that Madison and Hamilton lived in a world dominated by the work of Isaac Newton while Webster and Calhoun lived at a time when the newer science of geology had begun to make itself felt. By instinct, then, one generation thought more in terms of mechanical apparatus and the other more in terms of contingent building and collapse. Though both generations disagreed violently within themselves on how to make the political choices they confronted, both shared internally the deeper, often inarticulate terms out of which explicit premises and assumptions and arguments later got fashioned. It is at this deeper, hidden level that tradition does most of its work. Like the first,

nearly invisible layer of cannonballs on a courthouse
lawn, the maps we steer by condition and confer authority upon the shapes of things we are prepared—and
able—to see.

Contagious Knowledge

Tradition is, remember, a mode of knowing as well as
the content of what is known—that is, it provides a way
of thinking about the world that confers a powerful aura
of legitimacy on what gets thought. It is the self-justifying
matrix in which individual bits of memory sit and, as a
result, invisibly determines which bits will fit, which
not, and what happens to them when they get in place.
Managers at Alcoa, as at Ford and GM, long were confident that theirs was a domestic business. Chevy engineers were certain they knew how to design small cars.
Deere's Plow Works contingent had no doubt about who
could make the best hitches. They did not just think so.
They knew.

From the mid-1960s on, for example, RCA's most significant corporate research effort had to do with videodisc technology. Justifiably concerned that government
dollars for R&D would not keep pace with the costs of
staying at the forefront of advances in electronics, the
managers of RCA's Laboratories needed a project that
would have an indisputable call on the support of the
company's operating divisions. The videodisc, which was
to be the heart of a major new system of home enter-

tainment, was just such a project. Here is what happened:

> Mindful of earlier problems with the high cost of color television and anxious to shift the priorities of researchers who had done primarily non-commercial work, RCA's Laboratories' management emphasized for its videoplayer research projects rigid economic goals, rather than high performance goals. This led to the choice of a technological alternative, the capacitance approach, that was lower in cost, but also restrictive in its ability to support a range of performance options. General consultation that took place at the divisions about the product concept showed that the divisions thought performance features were more important than the Laboratories did, but the Laboratories insisted on retaining control over all technical decisions.
>
> Later, as RCA's competitors announced higher performance videoplayer alternatives, the project had to keep increasing its performance targets. Meanwhile, the RCA Consumer Electronic Division, which had never supported the Laboratories' choice of technology, pursued competing alternatives. In 1975, [that division] . . . having lost the internal flight over technological alternatives, decided to market a Japanese-produced videocassette recorder that proved to be a direct competitor to the internally developed Videodisc.[33]

Now, units within organizations always compete for turf, for resources, and for acceptable definitions of policies and priorities. Within limits and when carefully managed, such competition is probably a healthy thing. The history of RCA's experience with the videodisc, however, is a painfully familiar example of what can happen when internal competition bespeaks not a healthy jostling but a confused lack of fit between larger goals and local actions. The decision at the Laboratories to stick with the capacitance approach and, by extension, with its performance limitations, cut off some internal sources of support, pushed an important corporate outlet for the technology into the arms of a Japanese alternative, and prepared the ground for the videodisc's ultimate problems when it finally did reach the market some years later. Why, then, such devotion—and at such cost—to this particular technical approach? Why the denial of the appeal of competing approaches?

Why, indeed? The thing we get from the best modern study of the case is telling. For a variety of reasons, managers at the Laboratories wanted to be at work on a major technical project that allowed for rigid economic control. Fair enough, but what were those reasons? First, a concern to get researchers—who had been used to the financial "give" in government-funded work—quickly accustomed instead to the tighter cost goals of consumer product development. And, second, to avoid with this new home entertainment product the cost problems associated with RCA's past experience in color television. To practitioners, these reasons will probably make excellent sense. They are plausible and hardheaded. At the time, they must have seemed eminently sensible. Only armchair critics would fault them because only armchair critics enjoy the luxury of knowing beforehand how things turned out.

Well, let us leave the comfort of our chair for a moment and point out the particular form of horse holding going on at the Laboratories. The message that comes through loud and clear is that the experience with color television has left some scars and that managers do not want any repeat of the cost-based worries that dogged their work on that earlier technology. Videodisc is to be a major home entertainment system, as color television was. The basic technical choices it offers present, in turn, the opportunity for clear economic choices, just as color television did. Behind the explicit policy decision at the Laboratories lurks the half-hidden force of a powerful, virtually irresistible analogy. Not an extrapolation (like the giant, but impossible, flying ant of Chapter I), but another form of similitude: an analogy.

If we listen carefully, we ought to be able to hear the sound of cannonballs getting stacked somewhere. Grant the force of the analogy, and the mind-set that flows from it will structure and condition everything it touches. Accept the nagging inner fear that videodisc is color television yet again and not a different technology seeking a different market under different circumstances, and the way will be prepared to interpret every new bit of data, every twist and turn of the development effort, every idiosyncratic fact, as an unwanted repetition of earlier difficulties.

It is as if we were to sit down to translate a passage from some Latin text only to find a very rough and literal translation ready for us on the opposite side of the page. We would be more than human not to peek. Worse, because a handy trot is contagious, we would quickly find it hard to imagine ourselves doing without. Its idi-

oms and syntax rapidly infect our own. With nary a
warning, it has structured our very approach to translation. We think we are using the trot, but it is using us.

In organizations, contagious infection of this sort is a
more virulent mechanism still because the spectacle of
other people responding in the same fashion as we are
puts an end to residual doubt. No small part of the force
of tradition, of things known by being "passed on," is, as
we have seen, the common law legitimacy they carry.
Most organizations are, quite understandably, suspicious
of new ideas and will not easily adopt a new way of
looking at things. They are not quite so bad as the leg-
endary Boston potentates who have lunched for years at
Locke-Ober's, at the same table and at the same hour
and on the same menu items. But, at times, they come
close, for the reassuring warmth of shared and sustained
practice—whether at the table or at the level of idea—is
a mighty confirmation of the impulse to keep on doing
more of the same.

Think, again, of our Brahmin at his table, of how favorite waiters hover nearby, of how the rewarding smile
of the maître d'hotel says with quiet emphasis, Yes, indeed, this is as it should be. Where in this tableau of
comfort is there any argument for change, for thinking
that other luncheon arrangements might be better? Every polished inch of wood paneling argues the reverse.
Every additional meal entrenches the pattern further
and, more than that, the deep sense that the pattern is
right. Arthur Thornhill Sr., for years the head of Little,
Brown, always had a second Canadian Club on the rocks

before luncheon at Locke-Ober's. The day he died—
appropriately enough between drinks while at luncheon
at his regular table—the waiter brought his second drink
and left it there, untouched, for the rest of the day. In
the annals of such things, it was a signal honor.

Point to the white-haired dodderer at his midday scrod,
and we all smile at the comical if charming surface of
tradition. Point to the subtle influence of geological science, and the smile grows a bit more forced. Point to the
hold on managers of prior experience with color television, and the smile disappears entirely.

The Effects of Contagion

But these viruslike infections do have consequences, as
RCA's bout with the videodisc makes clear. They do not
sit quietly in a corner, barren of effect. Sometimes gent-
ly, sometimes with visible force, they condition the way
we view the world. Once we grant them tacit acceptance, they can show up to influence things in the least
likely places. Innocent they may seem, but their silent
power to affect our action and judgment is none the less
for that. Consider, in this light, the nature of the relation
both policymakers and managers typically assume to exist between science and technology. Consider, too, the
practical results of this assumption. John McKelvey, a
professor of physics at Clemson, puts the issue nicely:

> The oft-neglected fact, however, is that the development of
> pure science has not infrequently been enhanced by techno-

logical innovation involving little or no scientific input. Yet today our science and technology enterprise is highly structured around the conventional wisdom that technology's role is to capitalize on scientific results for human use.

If we have thought about these matters at all, most of us do carry about in our heads the notion that scientific discovery comes first and then technological effort begins to find ways to put discovery to practical application. This is so, in part, because scientists have generally written more and more effectively about the history of these developments than have their technologist brethren. Then, too, as both sorts of endeavor have lived through the modern era's gradual institutionalization of professional work, the interplay of cultural value and funding reality has tended to allocate positions of greater prestige to science. This tendency has, in turn, been accelerated and reinforced—given the needs of wartime, hot and cold—by the federal government's growing influence on the composition of private as well as public R&D. Whatever its complex sources, the assumption of science's primacy is by now as well established in the public mind as in institutional structures.

This assumption, however, has holes in it large enough to drive a semi through. McKelvey again:

It was in 1819 that [Hans Christian] Oersted found that the needle of a compass deflects when an electric current passes through a coil surrounding the device. Why 1819? Because by then it was possible, using "voltaic cells" (batteries), to set up a steady electric current in a circuit. The voltaic cell, however, was a purely technological innovation based on very little scientific understanding. Its origin lay in the discovery by the physiologist Luigi Galvani in 1786 that the muscles in the legs of dead frogs contracted when placed in a circuit containing dissimilar metal electrodes and an electrolyte. Galvani attributed this to an effect he called "animal electricity."

However, Alessandro Volta soon challenged this idea, suggesting that "galvanic action" was due to the contact between dissimilar metals. Although more reasonable, this idea was equally incorrect. Even so, in 1800, Volta succeeded in making a reliable battery using discs of dissimilar metals separated by pads moistened with a saline electrolyte.[34]

It would be another forty years after Volta's efforts before Michael Faraday could put together a valid scientific explanation of how such a battery worked. By 1819, however, Oersted had enough practical knowledge in hand to discover the magnetic field linked with an electrical current. The significance of this sequence is not that technology necessarily drives science but, more modestly, that it can and often has.

If we ignore such historical experience, if we forget that working versions of clocks and lenses, of telescopes and microscopes, of electric lighting and photography long preceded accurate scientific knowledge of their critical physical properties and processes, we may well be tempted to skew our current support of technical efforts in the wrong direction. In one guise or another, this type of skewing happens all the time. Infections of traditional belief have consequences.

What makes the infection so hard to fight is that most

of it rages completely out of sight. When we tacitly assume the primacy of science in making R&D allocation
decisions or when memories of color television lead us to
pick the capacitance approach in videodisc research, our
assumptions are not things we are able to talk about
openly. They are not very accessible to debate or discussion. Odds are, we do not even know they are there.
More to the point, we cling to them with a strength that
has to do less with objective assessments of their merit
than with the fact that we possess them through tradition. They have been mediated to us through our participation in specific institutional environments. They
have become part of our own self-definition.

In a sense, these assumptions are the kinds of things
we learned at our grandmother's knee. They sit too deep
for us to be aware of them as consciously held opinions.
Had we been born to the landed aristocracy of Victoria's
England, we would have found it easier to dissent from
our friends and neighbors on the value of sending troops
to South Africa than on the desirability of going into
trade or taking a managerial job in the City. Sending
troops to fight the Boers was an issue about which we
could have an opinion. Going into trade was something
we just knew wasn't done.

These infections are also hard to fight because prolonged exposure so conditions us to a particular view of
the world that we build elaborate networks of idea and
value to defend them. It is not just that some managers
at RCA allowed themselves to think of the videodisc as
color television come again. They were certain they were

right and, in their certainty, put resources, effort, and careers on the line. Having done so, of course, they were more reluctant than ever to think otherwise. No one in midocean is quick to find obvious, troubling flaws in the lifeboat so carefully examined and selected but a little while since. Traditional belief does not sit quietly in a corner minding its own business. Let it flourish, and it will gradually co-opt to its own ends what lies next to it and, then, what lies beyond. A whole elaborate system of Victorian family and social pressures stacked the balance against taking a job in the city; generations of leading-edge thought and practice argued mightily—and with prestigious institutional support—against the notion that technology could drive science. Indeed, the operation of what Thomas Kuhn has called "normal science"—that nexus of accepted questions to ask, positions to be filled, and topics to study—turns even the political apparatus of supposedly impartial professions or fields of study into an immensely rich medium in which the virus of tradition can propagate at will.

As such contagion spreads, it drives out awareness of whatever facts stand in its way. It is the sworn enemy of institutional memory. Consider: for all its recent celebration of self-made men and corporate swashbuckling, our culture harbors deep suspicions of big-time industry. Now and then, these doubts come to the surface and roil the waters of everyday life; most of the time, they lie silent and show nary a ripple. But they still do their infectious work. To confess on a college campus in the late 1960s that a job waited in a bank or consumer goods company was to risk instant social ostracism. In the mid-1980s, to confess on that same campus that no place on Wall Street waits or that no start-up venture occupies idle evenings and weekends is to court the image of an also-ran. Certainly, fashions change. Beneath the fashions, however, there is venerable strain in our culture that accepts the mom-and-pop grocery store on the corner as a quaint necessity but bridles at the cavernous reality of a steel mill or tractor plant. Even in the days, not so long ago, when a belching smokestack seemed a symbol of economic health and not a senseless provocation of the EPA, large-scale enterprise raised doubts.

Held up against the facts of the case, this deeply entrenched suspicion of bigness provides an instructive example of how tradition makes its presence felt. Bear with the details for a moment. This is not an insignificant tale. Traditional suspicions have done much to influence government policy, as well as public attitude, toward business for more than a century. A generation that has witnessed the breakup of the Bell system and a decade-long, if ultimately unsuccessful, suit against IBM has little cause to doubt the far-reaching power of such influence.

From the late nineteenth century on, the brute fact of consolidation in industry after industry has seemed to many observers prima facie evidence of a frontal attack on the public good. Whether that consolidation referred simply to the scale of operations or to the combination of different enterprises under the same corporate umbrella, in practice it meant bigness. And bigness was bad. There was plenty of evidence, of course, that the new, raw power of large-scale enterprise could work harm on fair competition and the larger interests of society. There was a sorry track record of specific excesses and violations of the public trust. But those who, like Justice Brandeis, were viscerally opposed to bigness in and of itself were not motivated just by concrete malfeasance of this sort. They cherished a democratic vision of a small town and small-scale America that stood in direct opposition to the might of these new industrial combinations.

What this traditional prejudice against bigness overlooked—the facts it drove out of sight and beyond recall—were the very real differences among such combinations. Virulent tradition blurs categories or draws their boundaries wrong. In some industries, there was a push toward horizontal modes of integration—that is, formal or informal arrangements among competitors for the purpose of shoring up or boosting profits and keeping a tight ceiling on production. Let's not get into any foolish price wars or glut the market, these companies told each other. If we're clever and stay in touch, there is plenty of money for all of us. In other industries, there was a push toward vertical modes of integration—that is, efforts to improve efficiency or to lock in scale economies at relevant points in the production process. In the businesses we're in, these companies told themselves, it makes no sense to try to operate on a tiny scale. How can we possibly compete if we build automobile plants that turn out only a few cars each year of steel mills that produce only a few tons?

From a distance, both horizontal and vertical growth may look pretty much the same—especially to those who are allergic to bigness in any form. But in terms of the realities with which managers deal, there is every difference in the world. As Alfred D. Chandler, Jr., has shown, there were certain kinds of activities—the refining of oil and sugar, for example, or the production of steel, automobiles, sewing machines, heavy farm equipment, and cigarettes—that simply required large-scale integration. Virtually all the firms involved in these activities, which Chandler's colleague Thomas McCraw calls center firms, were capital-intensive, technically advanced, marked by scale economies, and run by elaborate managerial hierarchies. This was and is true of center firms in all the industrialized economies, not just in the United States. To do what they must in order to survive, let alone prosper, these firms must integrate vertically to some degree. Their bigness was an inescapable result of who they are and what they do. Such were the facts of certain kinds of enterprise.

There were, however, other kinds of activities—furniture making, food service, automobile repair, and textiles—that did not require vertical integration for efficient operation, that did not enjoy major scale economies, and that were not so capital intensive. The firms here, which McCraw labels peripheral firms, were not unimportant to the national economy. They were peripheral not in their effects on employment or GNP but only in the sense that they flourished in industries where technical and competitive requirements permitted successful operations on a small scale. Adam Smith would have found them altogether familiar while he would have looked with puzzlement and concern at, say, US Steel.

These patterns, remember, are not unique to the American experience. As McCraw puts it,

> the striking similarities between industrial experience in the United States and in other market economies suggest strongly that the economic and technological characteristics of certain industries encourage them to assume either a center or a peripheral configuration and to maintain that configuration over a long period of time. These characteristics now seem much more important than do differences in legal systems or national cultures; in fact they appear to determine the relative size and organizational structure of firms within the industries represented.[35]

Bigness among center firms, therefore, if it derives from vertical integration and the need for large-scale operation, is often the natural result of technological and economic imperatives. It is understandable, legitimate, even necessary. If, however, it crops up in other places or for other reasons, then we may reasonably begin to ask questions. The answers may prove benign, but they may not. We know too much about the world not to expect some efforts to form combinations in restraint of trade. And we know too much about economic health to allow such combinations to flourish unchecked. Our task is to distinguish these two forms of growth from each other and to get the facts about each right—not let traditional assumptions push us to view industrial bigness as a single, undifferentiated fact. Tradition, remember, is no respecter of the boundaries between categories of things; its infection blurs the lines of distinction.

The Principle of Infection

When infected, we let tradition convince us of some underlying identity between things that appear outwardly the same. Or between things that remind us of each other. Or even between things to which we apply the same emotions. We know better, we know the facts, but still we ask ourselves, How is it possible for people in other groups, other societies to think the way they do? After all, they are people just like us. They face the same crises of life and death. They have the same raw material to work with. How, then, can they come out in such different places? How can they feel aggrieved if they are prevented from placing the body of a dead parent on a wooden scaffold open to the air or (not so long ago) unless they are able to sacrifice a young maiden to their gods? How can the elders of Codfish Center be as straitlaced as they are and still permit unmarried couples to court by bundling together under the covers in the same bed?

And we still catch ourselves thinking—despite the facts—that videodisc is color television yet again, that science continues to drive technology, and that all bigness in business is bad. In a boundless variety of ways, we let tradition confuse us, and we pay the price, often a hidden price, for our confusion.

Why so? Complain that the outcome of a baseball game was not as we remember it to be, and we can check the box score. Complain that our antitrust policy is not having the effect intended, and we can gather the industry data we need to check the accusation. Complain that our development work on the videodisc is not going the way we intended, and we can juggle timetables and personnel assignments. Complain that our R&D allocations are misguided, and we can run through our formulas again. Complain that we ought not to send troops to fight a questionable war on another continent, and we can debate the merits of our geopolitical calculations. But challenge the values and assumptions we learned, in one sense or another, at grandmother's knee, and we do not listen or hear. Confusion wrought by logic or fact we can, if we must, discuss. Confusion wrought by traditional belief is something else again.

Back in the days when theologians debated the freedom of the will, the most powerful formulation of the determinist position was that we can do what we will but cannot will what we will. That is, we can choose whether to act on the motives and promptings that lie uppermost in our minds, but we are powerless to determine which promptings and motives they will be. The modern disciplines of psychology and psychoanalysis translate that theological argument into secular terms: We can make conscious choices about things but cannot by sheer willpower determine how those choices will be shaped by unconscious forces. In our organizational, as in our private, lives, there is a powerful shaping of our thought

and action that largely takes place out of sight and beyond the reach of easy or intentional manipulation. In
institutional settings, much of what drives this process is
tradition.

As we have seen, the shared repetition of "things
passed on" confers a deep sense of rightness or fitness.
For all their rationality, economic organizations are just
another form of social group and no more immune than
any other to the blandishments of this aura of legitimacy.
In practice, the sense of legitimacy—the feeling that
things are as they should be—does not stay neatly in the
little crevices where it first takes hold. It spreads. Like
red wine spilled on a white linen table cloth, it progres-
sively colors more and more of the material within its
reach. With differently woven threads or different kinds
of material, the pattern and timing of the spreading stain
may vary. But spread it will. Traditional belief operates,
after all, as a kind of contagious viral infection. It changes
what it touches and changes next what lies beyond.

This principle of contagion is diagnostically important
because it throws into sharp relief the mechanism by
which tradition works its effects in an institutional context. As the infection speads, the view of things it helps
to structure takes in more and more of the world. A
language with no words for fish—and no ability to generate them—would show itself wanting as a language
when native speakers reach, as sooner or later they must,
river, lake, or ocean. When Captain Cook's party of sail-
ors saw their first kangaroo in Australia, they thought it
was a giant mouse. Untroubled confidence in our view of

things—which is central to the felt legitimacy of traditional belief—is possible only when our way of looking at
the world can effortlessly expand to cover new aspects of
that world, as they show themselves over time. By the
same token, of course, the more smoothly it can expand,
the more we are confirmed in our sense of its rightness.
Do the circumstances of the late nineteenth century
throw open to us a whole new level of industrial consolidation? Well, we know how to think about bigness in
business.

Still, how is it, we may reasonably ask, that the infection of traditional belief can maintain itself in the face of
ever more acccurate knowledge about the world? If the
facts are plain and we still misconstrue them out of some
perverse allegiance to an old wives' tale, then why not
write us off as dumb or superstitious or worse? When we
have the comparative data in front of us that distinguish
vertical from horizontal modes of integration, what possible explanation can we have for sticking with our knee-
jerk prejudice against bigness in general? Our Brahmin
at his noontime scrod strikes us at first glance as a creature of mindless, if comfortable, habit. If we determine
our antitrust policy or design our videodisc project in the
same fashion that he chooses a place to lunch, how can
we hold up our professional heads? We had better be
able to go behind our father's saying.

The ideas and attitudes of which we are aware—and of
which we are in fair control—lie close to the surface. Certainly, tradition may influence them strongly. We may
choose to set our holiday table the way grandmother did.

But the real work of tradition goes on at a deeper level, out of sight. The material through which it has its primary effect is not the kind of stuff that we can name or identify when asked. Rather, it is the stuff of our deepest, usually inarticulate assumptions, the categories with which we structure the world and make sense of it. It is what lies behind our instinctive sense, given a Victorian grandmother of the landed aristocracy, that a job in trade or in the City is unacceptable. It is what lies behind the mental itch that tells us to maintain tight economic control of our videodisc project.

By working through such material as this, tradition provides a contagious way of knowing the world. Tradition, remember, is self-legitimizing. It gathers strength and energy from its own exertions and profits from the mutual infection of all those within an institutional setting. We are not dumb or superstitious or irresponsible when we allow its contagion to touch us. We are merely human. And our organizations offer a congenial environment for its infection to spread. But we are not helpless. We have history, the power of institutional memory. We can add back the facts that have leached away. We can disrupt the engine of similitude.

II

So much for general description. What do these mechanisms of infection actually look like in practice? In 1916 Thomas Midgley, a mechanical engineer, joined Charles Kettering's industrial research laboratory, Delco, in

Dayton, Ohio, to work on the problem of engine knock in automobiles. As the threat of war and the nation's growing reliance on the automobile gave priority to the development of more powerful and efficient engines, knock became a still greater problem. This was because the easiest way to raise both efficiency and power was to increase an engine's compression ratio, and higher ratios made knock worse. Left untreated, as Kettering understood, that familiar metallic pinging could stop being an annoyance and virtually rip an engine apart.

Midgley's initial studies turned up an unsuspected fact. Contrary to expectations, contrary to the direction of past research, knock had less to do with the mechanical operation of an engine than with the fuel that engine used. Solving the problem, then, meant less emphasis on making engineering changes and more on research into the chemistry of fuels and the process of combustion. Ultimately, this work led to the use of tetraethyl lead in gasoline. It was the immense good fortune of General Motors, which took over Kettering's laboratory in 1920, that Midgley and his staff addressed the problem assigned them by refusing to accept on faith the convenient assumption that knock was essentially an engineering problem to be fixed by an engineering solution.

This refusal to go along with the conventional wisdom reflects, of course, a happy commitment to the empirical approach in technical work. But it also reflects a determination hard to sustain in practice. We tend to view things in the light of what we know best, what we know

how to do. The old parable of the blind men and the
elephant does not go far enough. Yes, each sightless
fellow will interpret the nature of the object he touches
by a process of inference from the part of the beast on
which his hands chance to fall. But each will, in addition,
think of how to deal with that object in terms of what he
best knows how to do: a barber, to trim it; a butcher, to
carve it; an architect, to rearrange its masses. To one
degree or another, we are all captives of the "surgeon's
rule": If we cannot cut it out, it does not exist.

We all define things by reference to what we know
and how we operate. We look, for example, at the industrial development of biotechnology as if it represented
yet another instance of the familiar pattern by which
technology-based industries evolve. In our reading and
talking and planning, biotechnology tells us much the
same developmental tale as semiconductors did a generation ago. The chip casts a long shadow and inclines us
to view the monoclonal antibody in its silicon image.

In fact, as current research indicates, the two industries are following quite different paths of evolution and
bear little structural relation to each other. The one is
mostly technology-, not science-, based, the product initially of work done in corporate laboratories, and its industry has been shaped by a process of fission nearly
biblical in its sequence of corporate begats. The other is
primarily science-based, closely linked to work done in
university laboratories and marked less by its structural
relation to Matthew 1 than by the crazy quilt of joint
ventures and equity participations that have shaped it

from the beginning. Still, the shadow of the chip is hard to dispel.

In the early days of the telephone, especially before the perfection of switching technology, there was considerable difference of opinion on how Mr. Bell's implement would best be used. Western Union, as we have seen, thought it would function as a local feeder mechanism for business communications that would properly flow by telegraph. Several entrepreneurs thought it would primarily be a means of broadcasting information and artistic performances to a wide audience from a single source. Indeed, in August 1876, one publication opined that it would be possible, sooner or later, to

> repeat on one or more pianos the air played by a similar instrument at the point of departure. There is a possibility here . . . of a curious use of electricity. When we are going to have a dancing party, there will be no need to provide a musician. By paying a subscription to an enterprising individual who will, no doubt, come forward to work this vein, we can have from him a waltz, a quadrille, or a gallop, just as we desire. Simply turn a bell handle, as we do the cock of a water or gas pipe and we shall be supplied with what we want. Perhaps our children will find the thing simple enough.[36]

By the late 1890s Budapest, Hungary, was the happy possessor of a "telephone-newspaper," which passed along music, drama, and news to an audience of some 6,000 subscribers.

Now, there is nothing odd about the fact that it is often not clear at the outset how a new technology will develop. No one could know for a certainty in the 1870s that the telephone would ultimately develop as a networking and not a broadcasting medium. The Budapest experiment made perfect sense. The point worth noting, however, is how easily the initial guesses took on the form suggested by known modes of communication. To the question of what to make of Mr. Bell's "electrical toy," the instinctive response was, in most cases, that the telephone was to be a means to extend and improve activities that were already familiar. It was to be another kind of telegraph, another kind of newspaper, another kind of concert. In retrospect it is easy to smile at the image of teenagers calling up Ma Bell for a direct link to some heavy metal stage show. Even so, a few decades after the Budapest party line reached out to its subscribers, the advent of commercial radio realized the same broadcasting possibilities inherent but not developed in telephony.

In our own time, banks and other providers of financial services are actively trying to puzzle out which technical combinations will lead to a viable business in home banking services. How will the link be established with individual households—through telephone wires and a modem, through cable and a TV screen, through personal computers? And how will nonnetwork entertainment reach the home—by cable, by satellite, on membership basis, on a fee-per-view basis? The situation with these technologies is really not that much different from the situation with telephony a century ago. Many business possibilities lie embedded in technologies that are themselves still very much in flux. Who can be sure how things will shake out? All that we can say with certainty is that the possibilities we are now exploring did not suggest themselves to us in a vacuum. They are modeled after things we know in other contexts.

When the makers of automated manufacturing equipment set about the task of designing industrial robots, most of them wanted their robots to have arms and hands that would function much as those of their human counterparts do. But why, we might ask, ought these pieces of machinery be designed on an anthropomorphic basis? Is it obviously and unmistakably the case that that is, after all, the most appropriate design goal? As an expert in the field reminds us, if what we want is a robot that washes dishes, we do not need to create some expensive elaborate, articulated, and waterproof servo-mechanism. We can simply drop by Sears and pick up an automatic dishwasher.[37] Yet when we think of robots, we think of mechanical people. It would be surprising if we did not. We reason by some principle of similitude with things we know.

When we go beyond our dishwashing robot and think about automating an entire factory, chances are our thoughts turn to notions of doing with machines alone what men had done with machines before. And of doing much the same things in much the same order. Did workers used to lift this heavy metal panel with a winch, move it on a dolly to that drop forge, and orient it carefully in place? Let us, then, purchase the equipment and software necessary to do that job automatically. Did workers used to clamp a half-assembled component with a special vise in order to do some tricky welding? Fine, let us figure out how to automate both clamping and welding. Did the work of fabricating and assembling a microwave oven require a certain set of steps in a certain order? Well and good, let us bring in the machinery to do all that automatically. The impulse, of course, is to introduce new technology into a system designed for people and not to redesign the system to accommodate what the technology can do.

When contexts are superficially alike, we are prone to treat what lies within them according to some rough principle of similitude. Quite often, as Ernest May has shown in the development of foreign policy, the perception of likeness and the action to which it gives rise are badly misleading. "In the early months of World War I," May notes,

> President Woodrow Wilson found himself involved in disputes with the British about American rights on the seas. The diary of his close friend, Colonel House, records the President as saying, "Madison and I are the only two Princeton men that have become President. The circumstances of the War of 1812 and now run parallel. I sincerely hope they will go no further." Having this perception, the President acted cautiously.[38]

Without demeaning Old Nassau's influence upon the world, we may reasonably doubt that it extends to the naval realities of wars a full century apart.

Yet Wilson's instinct is perfectly understandable. We, too, grasp quickly at modes of interpretation that bring novel things within the orbit of what we know and are comfortable with. The earliest commercial jet aircraft proved unstable at high speeds because they employed the same wing design as older propeller-driven aircraft. The world's first bridge made out of cast iron was constructed on the same design as the wooden structures that preceded it. The initial market predictions for plain paper copiers suggested that only a few government agencies and insurance companies might have need of them because no other kind of office needed more than three or four copies of any piece of paper—and those it could get with carbons. At the time, it was not easy to see that the availability of a new kind of copying performance or aircraft engine or bridge material might undercut past practice or principle of design. After all, another form of duplication or propulsion or construction material is just that: another form of something familiar. And we know how to think about familiar things. There is more than a bit of Old Nassau in all of us.

It is such a simple matter to let that bit of Princeton determine how we view things. Its influence, though, is hard to track, for it is usually indirect and nearly always contagious. Indeed, we may notice the spreading infection, but prove unable to identify its source. In a practical sense, the more widespread the infection, the less immediately obvious its point of origin. Consider, for example, the way in which many modern presidents have come to feel about the State Department, an organization that John Kennedy once likened to a bowl of jelly. Here is May, again, on the affairs of State:

Foreign service officers consistently predominated not only in missions abroad but also in the department at home. Reports from instructions to embassies were thus filtered by men and women who idealized ambassadors, whose own ambitions looked to heading a mission abroad, and whose prospects for promotion depended on the favor of seniors whom they were theoretically supervising. For historical reasons, the State Department became an institution oriented toward serving and supporting the missions rather than the Secretary of State or the President. In fact, its whole incentive system ran against helping people in Washington make clear-cut decisions which might run counter to advice from a mission or tie an ambassador's hands.[39]

Senior Washington officials who expected the department's apparatus to serve the interests of the White House as staff typically serves an executive were badly disappointed. No wonder Kennedy thought the place a bowl of jelly. It did not behave as he thought it should. It did not work silently and efficiently as an instrument of his purpose. Instead, it buffered and sidetracked and finessed.

Had Kennedy taken a career officer by the collar and demanded the reason why, that unlucky soul could probably admit to some intentional foot-dragging but would not be aware just how pervasive or systemic the mechanics of avoidance and deflection were. The sense of legitimacy and rightness in the values underlying departmental behavior would, by then, be part of the very air that poor soul breathed. It would seem natural and proper to implement those values at every turn. There might, of course, be some awareness that not everyone in Washington would be thrilled with the results, but there would certainly be a deep-set conviction that dissenters could go lump it.

In this imaginary tableau of angry recrimination and sullen defense, we may assume, quite safely, that neither collarer nor collaree would understand why things were as they were. One is frustrated and bitter; the other scared but unrepentant. Neither has on the tip of his tongue an appreciation of how the institutional history of the department has worked to lock certain attitudes and assumptions in place and give them the force of common law. Over time, as those assumptions and attitudes infect all the nooks and crevices of departmental practice, as they spread the contagion along all organizational circuits, the world viewed from within is inescapably seen through the haze of the fever. As viewed from without, the department looks obviously feverish, but the cause is unknown and the treatment unclear.

Driven by annoyance, external observers raise the cry of incompetence or sabotage. Thinking the fever normal and the charge unjustified, those on the inside dig in their heels even further. Both reactions, when viewed from neutral ground, make sense. Both reflect the ascription to a particular set of circumstances of a cluster of judgments and expectations that more properly belong elsewhere. Both mistake what lies before them. Neither can break the cycle of imprecation and defiance. Sound familiar? On whatever side we found ourselves, as tradition hardens, as its virus spreads, it becomes ever more important to see that that is what is going on. The impulse to categorize by rote—to jumble together new experience and well-entrenched precedent—is the Old Nassau in all of us.

We do it by treating different contexts and problems as if they were fundamentally alike. We see what we are prepared to see. If we think of problems as things that get solved once and for all, then we have a hard time with so-called piano tuner problems, the kinds of things that need to be adjusted over and over again. Troubled by its underwhelming performance, a major materials producer discovered that it was still pricing its products to gain incremental share although it had been the industry leader for years. It no longer needed to behave that way because it enjoyed a competitive position substantially different from that of thirty years earlier. But it had a pricing policy geared to those earlier circumstances, and it continued to follow it because, after all, it *had* a policy, once-for-all.

In much the same fashion, if we run a consumer appliance business and stubbornly persist in thinking of service costs as consisting only of the expense of replacement parts and labor, then we may be deeply puzzled by what is really happening out in the field. For some years, in fact, the largest service-related cost in GE's home refrigerator business was the cost of replacing the linoleum torn by repairmen when they moved long immobile units away from the wall. Our categories are not just convenient places to file away what we find out there; they do much to determine what it is we find or even think to look at. The mind-set confirmed in us by tradition is only one of many possible windows on the world.

The building industry in which an electrical contractor like LKC, Inc. (originally L. K. Comstock & Company) operated during the early years of this century bears not much more than a surface likeness to the industry today. Back then, owners of buildings hired an architect and a consulting engineer, who in turn supervised a contractor and all the subcontractors. Today, the owners, who are as likely to be real estate speculators as residents of the building, tend to be far more concerned about costs, tax abatements, and the details of tax policy than about architectural detail. Accordingly, the roles of consulting engineer and architect have grown together, leaving the general contractor a much wider field of responsibility.

Had an old-line operation like LKC, Inc. continued to wait on the pleasure of consulting engineers and not made itself into a specialty contractor that worked directly with the top management of utilities and industrial companies, it would likely have disappeared. Many of its early competitors did just that—in part because they never quite understood how greatly the structure of the industry had changed. On the surface, things continued to look more or less as they used to; underneath, they had drastically changed.

How is it possible for someone knowledgeable about an industry to miss such a change? A novice, perhaps, but an old veteran? We trip over the answer every day. The infection of tradition leads us to impose upon the world our preferred and familiar structures of understanding. When feverish, we see only what we are prepared to see. And seeing it gives us pleasure, a warm feeling of rightness and comfort. With such a disease, no over-the-counter remedy is potent enough to provide even symptomatic relief. To be effective, the medicine must be powerful, bitter, and remorseless.

In the years before 1907, AT&T thought its development efforts strong enough and its ability to acquire patents and inventions externally well-enough established that no major program of in-house research was necessary. In the opinion of management, the technology on which the telephone business rested was advancing—and would continue to advance—in clear directions at a leisurely pace. This mind-set, confirmed and reaffirmed by organizational goals, values, assumptions, and policies, deeply influenced the way AT&T managers viewed the world. They were slow, more than slow, to appreciate how vulnerable the company might be to technical change. According to Leonard Reich, who has studied the early years of Bell Labs, "Before AT&T would undertake an extensive research program, corporate management had to recognize the disruptive capabilities of unusual and often unforeseen technological variants." In other words, nothing much would change until the hold of tradition was loosened.[40]

Prying that hold loose did not happen easily or painlessly. It took the example of other industrial companies like GE and Kodak, which had set up research labs some years before. It took the ascendancy of a new top management team. And it took a grudging recognition that radio technology might seriously disrupt the patent basis of AT&T's telephone business. The will to read the situation in 1907 as a stable continuation of the situation ten years before was fiercely and fully grounded. Institutional tradition locked it further in place. Market success offered additional confirmation. So far had the infection spread that few within the company understood that there was any infection at all. Only external examples, new management, and indisputable progress on other technical fronts could together force the needed diagnosis into the open. A mild physick would not do.

So powerful is the engine of similitude, even at the individual level, that the contagion it spreads is terribly hard to root out. In his autobiography, Peter Drucker tells of an experience fairly early in his career when he went to work for Freedberg & Co., a merchant bank in London. "I had been working in the firm only a few weeks when Freedberg called me in," Drucker recalls.

"Richard Mosell hired you," he said, "and you are not my concern. But really, Mr. Drucker, you are much dumber and far less competent than you have any business to be." I was taken aback. Richard Mosell had praised my work lavishly every day. "What am I doing that I shouldn't do, and what am I not doing that I should do?" I asked. "I understand," said Freedberg, "that you used to do securities analysis for that London insurance company you worked for last year. Well, you are still doing securities analysis. If that is what we had thought you should be doing, we'd have left you working for the insurance company. We made you executive secretary to this firm—and you haven't given any thought to what you now have to do to make a contribution and earn your salary. Today is Friday. Come back on Tuesday and give me your program in writing."[41]

Unless shaken out of our habitual practice or immunized against it, we all share the same impulse to do what we know how to do and to interpret our environment in terms of what is familiar to us. Left to our own devices, we all do the equivalent of securities analysis. We all sit contentedly at the luncheon table in front of our equivalent of the Brahmin's midday scrod. Pushed to change, our knee-jerk response is to define our new challenges as just another version of the tasks we know. That's us at the table, with a forkful of broiled fish halfway to our mouths. And with our free hand, we are holding a horse.

III

Understanding the mechanisms of contagion is only the first step. Next, of course, comes the effort to figure out how best to break the fever and stop the infection. What can we do in our institutional lives to loosen the hold of tradition? Must we trust to luck, divine intervention, or private revelation, or is there a pragmatic course we can follow that gives fair promise—albeit no guarantee—of such deliverance? If the only answer is, Yes, pay attention to history, that does not leave us with all that much to go on. Surely, the work of tracking down idiosyncratic facts and re-creating through memory how things really were before we imposed our categories on them is important. As a call to action, it is unobjectionable. But as a *basis* for action, for dealing with the here-and-now of current circumstances, it leaves much to be desired. Just what is it we *do* when we determine that the time has come to make ourselves the possessors, not the prisoners, of our past? How do we shake the fever and come into our inheritance?

These questions demand a response at two different levels. Both are important. The first has to do with the techniques of analysis we use when we turn our hands to the task of formal decision making. How should we think about whether to establish an independent R&D laboratory? What constraints should we place on a given new product development effort? What agenda of issues should dominate our attempts to solve a tricky technical problem? On what basis should we establish our pricing policy? What criteria should guide us as we think about the likely market response to new dimensions of product performance? The practice of management and curricula of business schools are chockablock with techniques to support these critical decisions.

To these approaches, however, must be added not another formal mode of analysis but, rather, a generally accessible means for becoming aware of the relevant history. It cannot be something that only experts or adepts can use, nor can it be so complicated that its value must be taken on faith. It has to be handy, reasonable, filled with common sense. It should not promise the moon and therefore bring on a cascade of disappointment, but offer merely to improve the quality of decisions at the margin.

Luckily, the beginnings of such an approach do exist and are readily available.

Drawing on their research and teaching at Harvard, Richard E. Neustadt and Ernest R. May have recently published *Thinking in Time: The Uses of History for Decision Makers* (New York: Free Press, 1986), which offers a handful of small *m* methods for taking account of history in making decisions. These methods range, for example, from separating information about an event or set of circumstances into what is known, unclear, and presumed to doing a minihistory of the people with whom one has to deal, a history that helps "place" them in terms of their own experiences and likely view of things.

No need, then, to dwell on this first level of response. Read the Neustadt and May book. It is the second level that requires our attention: building up a capability for recognizing day-to-day both the artifice that surrounds us and the effects that it has on us. Here, too, there are practical, commmonsensical guides. Moments of grave threat or crisis can, of course, rip away the veil of inattention and ignorance and force managers to confront their own comfortable assumptions. As we have seen, without a new team at the top who saw the threat posed by radio to the underlying logic of the telephone business, AT&T would not have made the organizational commitment it did to serious in-house R&D. But such moments are rare, thankfully so, and often come too late for timely action. Moreover, a policy of waiting for or, worse, encouraging potential disaster to unlock old modes of thought is a rather dangerous policy. It is brinkmanship of the most irresponsible sort. Yes, it is good to be able to learn from a crisis, but it is hardly desirable to foment calamity for the sake of what we can learn from it. Not many of us can so nicely control what we let out of Pandora's box.

We need not, however, purposely stray so near the brink. Instead, we can set ourselves the task of looking on a regular basis for those places where our accustomed explanations for things do not hold so well. That is, we can look for the spots in which the artifice we have otherwise forgotten frays around the edges. These signs of inadequate or incomplete "fit" give the game away—in that they forcibly remind us that what lies before us is, indeed, something constructed, something "built." Stephen Jay Gould puts it nicely:

> Remnants of the past that don't make sense in present terms— the useless, the odd, the peculiar, the incongruous—are the signs of history. They supply proof that the world was not made in its present form. When history perfects, it covers its own tracks.[42]

Such remnants are all about us and peek out, now and then, from the least expected corners. We need to be prepared to see them for what they are, not dismiss them as minor annoyances or irrelevant detail. Once we understand that such odds and ends are important, we can begin to backtrack, take new bearings, call old assumptions into question. They give us the occasion for critical reflection. Thomas Kuhn has shown us in his *The*

Structure of Scientific Revolutions that our broad theories of the world, our paradigms, do not as a rule give way all at once. They wear out in spots, slowly, incrementally, as observers note in this or that place how something shows through that the current paradigm cannot explain. In much the same way, the remnants for which we cannot easily account offer prime evidence of a gap in our thinking, a rip in the fabric of our certainty. Dealing fairly with them means holding that certainty once more up to the light. And that, of course, is when artifice and the workings of tradition become visible.

Does our pricing policy not seem to work any longer? Well, we can blithely assume that the policy is fine but that we are implementing it poorly, or we can go back and have a close look at the thinking on which that policy rests. Do we suddenly notice that two members of our artillery unit are behaving strangely as the gun goes off? Well, we can ignore it or take the time to find out precisely what they are doing—and why. Has our approach to building small cars not had the success we anticipated? Well, we can write it off, or we can try to understand just why it is we went about things in the way we did. Is our domestic orientation proving troublesome? Well, we can curse loudly about unfair trade practices in Japan, or we can ask ourselves just why it is we were so domestically minded in the first place.

Left to their own devices, the mechanisms of tradition will chug along unimpeded. To stop them in their tracks, to halt the spread of contagion, we must learn not to leave tradition alone. How to do this? Be alert to the appearance of remnants; search for signs of fraying; notice those places where the "fit" between assumption and experience shows evidence of giving way. A formal methodology? Hardly. But it is something we can all do. And it works.

Paul Fussell, one of the most thoughtful students of World War I, has taken a careful look at how the unprecedented experience of that war violated the language, the terms and concepts, with which people tried to talk about it. Sadly enough, the taking up of arms was and is nothing new in the annals of peoples and nations. Even so, the scale, the conditions, and the slaughter of the Great War utterly transcended what had gone before. New and frightening experience outdistanced the common ability to describe, categorize, understand. According to Fussell,

> The Great War took place in what was, compared with ours, a static world, where the values appeared stable and where the meanings of abstractions seemed permanent and reliable. Everyone knew what Glory was, and what Honor meant. It was not until eleven years after the war that Hemingway could declare in *A Farewell to Arms* that "abstract words such as glory, honor, courage, or hallow were obscene beside the concrete names of villages, the numbers of roads, the names of rivers, the numbers of regiments and the dates." In the summer of 1914 no one would have understood what on earth he was talking about.[43]

Men could still march toward the enemy lines, kicking a football in front of them as if they were embarked on the greatest sporting event of their lives, thinking of their task in a nearly feudal language sprinkled with gallant warriors and valorous foes. It took only a brief, brutal exposure to Ypres and Verdun, Passchendaele and the Somme, to break through that old vocabulary forever. As a character in one of Scott Fitzgerald's novels was later to say, these were battles that used up a centuries-long heritage of culture and belief. They were battles that

> took religion and years of plenty and tremendous sureties and the exact relation that existed between the classes. . . . You had to have a whole-souled sentimental equipment going back further than you could remember. You had to remember Christmas, and postcards of the Crown Prince and his fiancée, and little cafés in Valence and beer gardens in Unter den Linden and weddings at the mairie, and going to the Derby, and your grandfather's whiskers.[44]

All this was true. Not yet knowing the horrors of which this century would prove capable, the men who fought the Great War flung themselves at it in a cultural battle dress that could not withstand what it discovered. Old language buckled in impotence and despair. These are somber thoughts, to be sure, but they lay out with stark clarity what can happen when inherited tradition is rudely brought to bay by a confrontation with enormous new realities. When the clash is too abrupt, too catastrophic, it can rend a whole social fabric. It can cut apart entrenched institutions, institutions that have long seemed permanent, the way a sharp, hot knife cuts through butter. No matter how widespread the contagion of tradition, there are crises that can stop in its tracks and purge it ruthlessly from the system.

For those entrusted with management of such institutions, however, the challenge is not to imagine the kind of dynamite that will blast open ideas and practices long clogged by stubborn tradition. Explosives of the right degree of power are always available. Top corporate managers can always close down every facility in sight and fire subordinates by the hundreds or thousands. They can sell off divisions and abandon whole lines of business. They can, if they choose, slim down drastically and lop off many increments of capacity. They can shake their organizations to the core. Any fool in a corner office can blast things apart. What professionalism requires, instead, is the competence to judge how far to go before there is nothing left worth having. In the abstract, there is no difficulty in calling a halt to the spread of tradition. In practice, the trick is to find a medicine strong enough to cure but not so strong that it will also kill the patient.

Finding it is something we make harder for ourselves than it has to be. For our sins, we live in a time of great impatience. As our pundits tell us, we are profoundly influenced by television, and our span of attention in most matters is a good deal shorter than that of past generations. We are surrounded by the apparatus of instant communications and have seen our expectations about the speed with which knowledge gets shared grow far more demanding than those of an earlier age. The commander-in-chief able to speak in real time to the

front line general several continents away may find it
difficult to recall how long it used to take for even vague
rumors that a battle had started to filter back to civilian
leaders. Old Hickory, Andrew Jackson himself, first
leaped into national prominence by fighting the battle of
New Orleans—two weeks, in fact, after the war that
prompted it had ceased. Word had simply not yet reached
him.

These broader cultural changes have not passed the
corporation by. Early New England shippers used to
wait for months to hear whether their cargo had reached
its destination safely. It took even longer for an investment banking syndicate to close its books on a large new
flotation like the one that created US Steel. Today, of
course, this kind of information is virtually instantaneous.
So much is obvious and familiar. What we often lose
sight of, however, is that such great speed in one area of
endeavor builds silent expectations of comparable speed
in others. If a few keystrokes at a New York terminal can
change the maturities of a billion-dollar portfolio in Saudi
Arabia, why in the name of all that gladdens a CEO's
heart can we not get that factory in Bloomington up to
speed on our new product line?

The logic here is thin to the point of invisibility. But
that is not really the issue. Reasonable or not, expectations about the ease and rapidity of organizational change
have practical consequences. In the managerial gut, a
hunger for quick results breeds endless frustration with
corporate bowls of jelly. And frustration, in turn, breeds
a willingness, even a wish, to cut at once through all the

gloppy nonsense, shake things up, and get on with the task at hand. Where the system is clogged with the debris of tradition, where the injunction to change bogs down in layer upon layer of stockpiled hitches, the impulse is to consult an explosives expert. What, those guys in Bloomington are dragging their heels? Well, we'll see about that.

In our better moments, we remember that, in virtually all institutional settings, sophistication of analysis quickly outruns ability to implement. As the history of strategic planning reminds us, getting the analysis right is conspicuously less than half the battle. Still, hard plans do sink into soft resistance and often disappear without a trace. Look out over the swamp of corporate efforts to restructure and adapt to changed terms of competition. Those widely spaced bubbles mark the places where elegant strategic formulations went down for the third and last time, weighted heavily by the pendulous trappings of tradition. Had we but cut the cord or blasted away the restraints, we wonder, would those plans have had a chance?

The managerial hand may itch for the knife or the blasting cap, but there is good reason not to scratch too quickly or too deeply. As with other kinds of infection, drastic scratching may only spread the problem. And radical intervention may do more lasting harm than good. As we have seen, a vital tradition can nourish and sustain levels of teamwork, commitment, inner-direction, and motivation that are hard to replace. We can, if we choose, forcibly excise the thick encrustations of "things passed on" that surrounds the operation of the nation's military. But will doing so make our armed forces more effective? Chances are, those buys in Bloomington have an excellent reason for doing what they do. At the same time, of course, we cannot let ourselves be governed by their intransigence. As Yul Brynner proclaimed on several thousand nights, "Is a puzzlement."

What to do? Left to its own devices, the engine of similitude through which tradition operates will capture and co-opt the way we think about new ideas and initiatives. Stopping that engine in its tracks is possible, but at huge cost. Knowledge and awareness can throw up a roadblock. We can, as Mark Twain did in his steamboating years, learn to read and thus master the language of the river. But we, like Twain, stand to lose something of great value. Returning contentedly to our midday scrod is not a legitimate option. But neither is scattering a truckload of high explosives through the dining rooms at Locke-Ober's. Is a puzzlement.

Well, not necessarily. Tradition is, as we've been talking about it, both a kind of knowledge and mode of knowing. It has a certain content, built up over the years, which is self-legitimating and which infects and conditions the way new experience gets apprehended. Videodisc? Ah, yes, we know how to think about that. We lived through the development of color television. More efficient automobile engines? Ah, yes, it must be an engineering problem. Industrial robots? Yes, again, we must build them to duplicate human abilities. In each case, the juggernaut of similitude, of contagion, lumbers in a wrong direction. The well-oiled rail on which it runs—the mode of traditional knowing—works just fine. It is the content that plays us false, gives us a mistaken heading.

Our experience teaches that what is truly valuable to us in tradition is its manner of operation—the way it generates legitimacy, commitment, allegiance, and a deep sense of being centered. All this we would hate to lose. What is troublesome is its blind, mechanical devotion to inappropriate or outdated content—the virus that can infect but that does not really belong in new situations or contexts. To be free of the latter, as we should, must we give up the former as well? To become aware of the mechanics, as we must, do we also have to sacrifice the social and institutional values of approaching the world in a traditional way? In a word, no.

Unlike the primitive and premodern societies that depended for survival on unquestioned obedience to tradition, modern institutions like the corporation have the ability to become aware of their own history, their own existence in time. This is no small point. From this sort of knowledge, there is no going back, no retreat to innocence. With it, there is no excuse for inaction. The poet W. H. Auden had a clear understanding of what this kind of modern awareness meant. "If we talk of tradition today," he wrote,

> we no longer mean what the eighteenth century meant, a way of working handed down from one generation to the next; we

mean a consciousness of the whole of the past in the present.
Originality no longer means a slight modification of one's immediate predecessors; it means the capacity to find in any
other work of any date or locality clues for the treatment of
one's own subject-matter.[45]

True, Auden was writing in the context of the materials
available to the twentieth-century poet in addressing the
concerns of twentieth-century life. But his argument has
broader applicability. In terms of access to tradition, what
sets today's manager off from the chieftain of an ancient
tribe is that the poor fellow in loincloth or robe had no
ability or opportunity to choose what it was that served
his people by way of cultural cement. He could muster
no critical distance. What was there was there. That was
all there was, and so it had to be preserved.

In the corporate world, however, there *is* a possibility
of choice and selection, the opportunity to cast a thoughtful eye over all the things that a company has been or
done during its existence. We *can* search for remnants,
for the pieces that do not fit, for the places where explanations fray. Consequently, there is a possibility of shaping the tradition that invisibly shapes things in the
present. Things will still get handed down or passed on
in the old way, of course. And that very process will still
give them a powerful aura of legitimacy. But—and this is
the nub of the matter—managers with a knowledge of
company history, managers with a vital connection to
institutional memory, have access in the present not just
to what has survived the generations of sifting and trans-

mission. *All* the past is available to them. They need not kill the patient to cure a specific disease or remove a specific constraint. Remember, in both personal and institutional terms, all the circuitry, the wiring, is in place, ready to pass the contagion along. History does not offer freedom or immunity from the mechanics of infection. But it does offer some basis for managing what kind of infection it is to be.

IV

The Steamer Trunk in the Attic

Antiquity, like every other quality that attracts the notice of mankind, has undoubtedly votaries that reverence it, not from reason, but from prejudice. Some seem to admire indiscriminately whatever has been long preserved, without considering that time has sometimes co-operated with chance; all perhaps are more willing to honor past than present excellence; and the mind contemplates genius through the shades of age, as the eye surveys the sun through artificial opacity. The great contention of criticism is to find the faults of the moderns, and the beauties of the ancients. While an author is yet living, we estimate his powers by his worst performance, and when he is dead we rate them by his best.

—SAMUEL JOHNSON

LIVING IN HISTORY, as we all do, like it or not, forces us to wrestle with an uncomfortable paradox. To have access to the energies and commitments that come only with a vital connection to our past, we must participate in the operation of tradition. To participate in that tradition, however, binds us to a very limited version of

151

our past—a version that often saps commitment and energy because it does not speak to the needs of present circumstances. What to do? We must, somehow, find a way to loosen the bonds of tradition—but loosen them selectively—and then reattach them to new and different objects. This is, of course, much easier said than done.

Chapter III suggests a place to begin. First, by looking for remnants, for places where familiar explanations do not adequately cover the facts or where bits and pieces of traditional apparatus show through, we can make ourselves once more aware of the artifice about us. Once we do this, we can then begin to win our freedom from the blind hold of tradition, of "things passed on." Complete freedom, however, is something we should neither seek nor desire. There is much in tradition, we must remember, that enriches our lives and institutions, and we ought not be so quick to wish it blasted out of existence. The real value for us lies in becoming aware of the conventions and categories that shape our view of things, not in reflexively consigning them to the ash heap—even if we could. Knowing artifice for what it is is the first step in gaining access to *all* of our past, to *all* of what lies buried in institutional memory, not just to that sifted portion passed on to us by the common law operation of contagious belief.

Such is the argument of the last chapter: We must learn how to read the language of this particular river. In practice, however, the discovery of artifice often short-circuits the step-by-step, selective process of forging access to a more ample past. It is common, indeed, for such a discovery to prompt a determination to yank tradition out, root and branch. Mad at ourselves for having been held in invisible fetters for so much time, we are prone to say, A pox on all these shreds and patches. Let us start afresh, with a clean slate. Let us build from scratch. No selective loosening of bonds here. In fact, quite the reverse. Shocked by the discovery of just how many ropes tie us down, we are impatient with the thought of undoing them one-by-one and find intolerable the notion that we ought to leave some of them as they are. Our impulse is to look for a sharp knife, and our long-term plan is to bury the severed strands out of sight.

In this final chapter we move toward a more constructive response. After an initial reminder of just how powerful our need for tradition is, we distinguish two different aspects of tradition—the parts with utility and the parts that are there for show. The latter, it turns out, change very slowly indeed, given the strong hold they maintain on our emotions. These emotions, however, can be displaced onto new objects and can be made to support new ends. This is all to the good, for almost every tradition contains a wide stockpile of unused items, some of which might well be suited to current need—if, that is, a way could be found to enlist emotional support for them. Taken together, the rummaging about for unused pieces of tradition and the displacement onto them of our loyalty and commitment are what the "management" of tradition is all about. No need, then, to throw away the whole kit and caboodle.

No more than the rest of us do managers like to be reminded of how they have been gulled, led astray, or made to wear blinders. A generation and more of bad decisions at US Steel cannot be remedied by changing the corporate name to USX, but there is obviously some hope that the new appellation will lead recollection away from those decisions and the thinking that led to them. Believing that tradition has tricked us, played us false, we do not want to hear about what it has to offer if we pick our way through it selectively. What we think we want is to be free from all such inherited baggage. We are confident that calling ourselves USX is the path to unencumbered freedom. We are wrong.

In the first place, even when we see the "built" character of our world and of the maps by which we steer in it, we cannot entirely do without tradition. The past shoulders its way into our present with the same inexorable force that creates a new mountain range out of a previously flat landscape. We possess—and require—a vital, contagious linkage with what has gone on before—no matter how strongly we may deny it. In fact, if it does not exist richly enough for us, we create it. In the political world, the totalitarian and utopian movements that have most actively sought to cut their lives with the past have rapidly—and intentionally—developed binding traditions of their own. Bolshevism was supposed to be something new under the sun; May Day has become a venerable institution. Close to home, today even Cabbage Patch dolls come with their own birth certificates.

Examples of this phenomenon abound. The American

national anthem has been the national anthem for only half a century. Before 1740, there were no national anthems anywhere. Before the 1790s, there were few truly national flags. These essential trappings of modern life had to be invented, fairly recently at that, as did the historical charter for the nation states they have come to represent. Linkages back to a credible past we must have, one way or another. Not long ago, personal computers were broadly seen as high-tech products suitable only for a small population of whiz-bang technical experts. Now they are broadly perceived as consumer products much like any other—products that enjoy the feeling of long-standing acceptance conferred by sentiments of brand loyalty. This loyalty may be of short duration in real time, but it rapidly takes on the aura of long-lived acceptance. At need, then we will invent such backward-looking connections. It is hard for us to find secure footing in a world where the turtles do not run all the way down.

Much as we say we wish to be altogether free of the tiresome effort of stockpiling hitches—linkages to the past—such radical freedom is really not for us. In practice, it would make modern institutional life impossible. Hitches there must be. As the historian Eric Hobsbawm reminds us, "Nothing appears more ancient, and linked to an immemorial past, than the pageantry which surrounds the British monarchy in its public ceremonial manifestations. Yet . . . in its modern form it is the product of the late nineteenth and twentieth centuries."[46] We ought not be surprised. Taken too far, of course, the work of establishing some effective continuity with the past, even a carefully and consciously selected past, can lead to a whole stable's worth of horse holding. Even so, deeply felt continuity is of such overriding importance that we must run the risk. Without such a linkage in place, without a goodly supply of hitches, present arrangements would lack the aura of legitimacy they need to enlist our commitment and loyalty.

The British made a deliberate choice, Hobsbawm tells us, when they rebuilt their Parliament building in the nineteenth century in the Gothic style. Their decision was "equally deliberate . . . after World War II to rebuild the parliamentary chamber on exactly the same basic plan as before."[47] These were not just aesthetic judgments about what would nicely catch the eye. They were careful reaffirmations of a much deeper vision of national and institutional identity. In corporate as in national life, the choice is not between a barren, amnesiac present and the straitjacket of the past. Experience tells us that it is, indeed, possible—within limits—to define the past that in turn defines our present. We *can* make selections from all that the past has to offer. What we possess through tradition is something that we ourselves *can* help shape.

Doing Versus Showing

Important as it is to realize that we are able, to some extent, to manage the past, we must not forget the kind of thing with which we are dealing. Those of us who have

suffered through the recent outpouring of books and ar-
ticles on corporate culture have reason to be allergic to
such forgetfulness. Genial instructions to change an organization's culture to fit new circumstances may play
sweetly upon the ear. But they reflect little understanding of just what it is that can be changed by good management—or how. The good news is that linkages with
the past do not lie entirely beyond our control. The bad
news is that we had better be pretty darn careful in
identifying those pieces to which the good news applies.

Even in the most conservative institutions, changes
that make practical sense go far toward justifying themselves. The most right-wing think tank in Washington
will not prohibit electronic word processing in favor of
old-fashioned quill pen, ink, and blotting paper. Far from
it. Nor will the conservative, old-time manufacturer of
industrial fasteners turn up its collective nose at a new
software program for accounts receivable. Hobsbawm
again:

> Wearing hard hats when riding [horses] makes practical sense,
> like wearing crash helmets for motor-cyclists or steel helmets
> for soldiers; wearing a particular type of hard hat in combina-
> tion with hunting pink makes an entirely different kind of
> sense. If this were not so, it would be as easy to change the
> "traditional" costume of fox-hunters as it is to substitute a
> differently shaped helmet in armies—rather conservative in-
> stitutions—if it can be shown to provide more effective pro-
> tection. . . . The spurs of Cavalry officers' dress uniforms are
> more important for "tradition" when there are no horses, the
> umbrellas of Guards officers in civilian dress lose their signif-

icance when not carried tightly furled (that is, useless), the
wigs of lawyers could hardly acquire their modern significance
until other people stopped wearing wigs.[48]

Tradition, then, is not made up of a single kind of stuff.
Some parts of it have—or had—practical applications;
other parts are there just for show. This distinction has
consequences. "Things passed on"—whether object or
idea—that are of immediate practical application are
fairly vulnerable to replacement by new things, by other
selections, that work better. Not always, of course, but
much of the time. This is not to say that change will be
painless or immediate, only that it is reasonably possible. Nor is this to suggest that change, once made, will
not have troubling and often unforeseen side-effects.
New army helmets that are not good for cooking or wash-
ing in will put additional demands on other pieces of
standard field equipment. "Things passed on" that lack
such utility change much more slowly.

In the world of affairs, performance matters. No manager of an assembly plant will enjoy a long and fruitful
career if that career is spent in stubborn resistance to
new processes or approaches that everyone can see are
preferable to the old. Grizzled veterans can, of course,
deflect the threat of the new by a thousand varieties of
foot-dragging and outright sabotage. But when the organizations for which these veterans work are convinced of
the merits of the changes the veterans are so cleverly
resisting, that resistance becomes itself a visible problem

for management to deal with. Demonstrable utility is its own best argument: It creates pressure for change.

By contrast, "useless" spurs, umbrellas, wigs, styles in hunting caps, and the like are less amenable to change, less able to create organizational pressure, because their purpose is different. They are not there to *do* something but, rather, to *show* something. As a result, they have nothing to do with greater efficiency or effectiveness. The impossibly long fingernails of the Confucian mandarin were meant to advertise his brute separation from all manual labor. The impossibly tight corsets of proper Victorian ladies were meant to advertise much the same thing—decorative ornaments, as these ladies were, of their husbands and paramours. Thorstein Veblen has sketched out this case better than anyone else: Consumption becomes truly conspicuous only when its object is for show and not to satisfy mundane need. Reserving parking spaces or private dining rooms for top-level executives is not a practice designed to boost performance. It is a means of social display, of saying something.

It is hard for us to tell—and harder to remember— which pieces of our traditions are meant for action and which for show or statement. But it is very important that we do so. If we do not, odds are we will either waste precious time and energy trying to change what we cannot or make only cosmetic adjustments that we mistakenly believe go to the heart of the matter. Shaking up a stodgy traditional factory by bringing in robots is, surely, a visible "hardware" approach to manufacturing problems. But it makes little sense if this new technology is only something to brag about, not something that addresses underlying problems. In much the same way, we make a great mistake when we confuse the reason for resistance to new technology: Is it born of knowledgeable suspicion about the staying power of front-office initiatives? Or is it resistance that is merely pigheaded?

We experience the separate strands of tradition not as isolated things but as parts of one large, gloppy, and undifferentiated whole. The old-line factory managers who drag their feet at the prospect of installing robots rarely do so as a matter of blind defiance. As a rule, they have reasons, plausible-sounding reasons, for their hesitation and copious justification for their delay. Often, they themselves do not know precisely why they object to the proposed changes: They just feel wrong. It is no easy matter to sort through these resistances, explicit as well as implicit, and tell for certain which reflect honest disagreement about how things would work and which hostility to what the changes would mean or symbolize.

When, indeed, do hard hats stop being practical and start being symbolic or expository? How much of the way an office is arranged is meant to say something? At what point is RCA's capacitance approach to videodisc technology more an expression of economic toughmindedness than of the wish to solve a set of technical problems? It is not easy to tell. We are hard pressed to define just how far our interest in things depends upon their utility—and utility only. Nor do we readily know how to construct such definitions.

But such definitions matter. We need to know just where in our traditions there is any "give"—any realistic hope of making practical alterations. We need to know where new purpose can turn old means to advantage. Tough as these definitions are to construct, we simply must have them—have an accessible mode of getting or building them—or else not be able to choose with any care which knots in the traditions that bind us we have a real chance to untie. The trouble is, however, that when we turn our attention to this sort of task, we often make the problem worse.

First of all, we find it terribly difficult to get all the pieces of a vital tradition laid out on a table for observation and discussion. We know them when we see them, but we have the devil's own time trying to draw up a complete list of them out of the blue. Ask even the dullest boy in a sixth-grade class to offer definitions of common words beginning with the letter k, and the chances are he will do just fine. Ask him to list all the words he can think of that begin with k, and the list will prove rather short. All of us know more than we can think of to say. We need hooks of some sort to pull up from memory all of what we know.

This is what Michael Polanyi meant by the "tacit" quality of knowledge, especially the kind of professional knowledge on which managers rely. "We know a person's face," Polanyi reminds us, "and can recognize it among a thousand, indeed among a million. Yet we usually cannot tell how we recognize a face we know." And if we try to break the problem down into little pieces, we often just stump ourselves. "By concentrating attention on his fingers," Polanyi argues, "a pianist can temporarily paralyze his movement."[49] In such matters, the fiercer and more restricted our gaze, the more likely we are to miss what we want to see. Stare fixedly at a luminous dial in the dark, and the hour we stare at will disappear. Ask pointedly about the traditional sources of our approach to the videodisc or small car design or pricing policy, and there will be uncomfortable silence.

Much of what we know through tradition is not easily broken down into plain statement or plain fact. We know it pretty much by feel. In the old days of soap making at Procter & Gamble, the men responsible for mixing the soap and seeing to it that what came out of the vats was as it should be—these men would often pull a curtain around themselves as they did their final checking. Theirs was a special, highly prized skill. Only they were allowed to know the mysteries of getting things just right. They did their work by sight, by touch, and by taste. They knew a faulty batch the way an expert gardener knows something is wrong in the azalea bed. They did not have to consult a manual. They just knew.

Not surprisingly, the soap made in one plant often bore little relation to the soap made in others—or, for that matter, to soap made in the same vats and kettles a week or a month before. P&G's great achievement in the early part of this century—and the first major application of its new commitment to R&D—was to get these processes under control. Today it seems perfectly obvious that when the appropriate managers sign off on the formula card for a product and on the specs for its manufacturing process, every unit produced should be just like every other. When we buy a bar of Ivory, we do not expect to be able to tell it from a bar produced three months before at a different plant.

We have come to take this utter predictability for granted. Yet it represents a significant accomplishment: breaking down a problem—like that of getting batches of soap to turn out consistently the same way—into its constituent parts and naming them. Making tacit knowledge explicit is a significant achievement. It is an important part of the process by which the useful portion of tradition gets translated into terms that managers can apply. Indeed, it lies at the heart of sound management. The glory of twentieth-century manufacturing, after all, is not really the discovery of Henry Ford's moving assembly line. Shipbuilders in fifteenth-century Venice had much the same idea. It is, rather, the reduction to consistent, predictable, and replicable practice—to utility—of what had been the idiosyncratic work of artisans, craftsmen, and engineers. It is making explicit the full content of traditional practice and so opening it up to study, systematization, and purposeful change.

In the old kettle house at P&G, there were pipes that ran from everywhere to everywhere, generations of pipes that had built up much the way a coral reef does. No one really knew which ones did what. All they knew was that, en masse, the piping worked. On the wall was a large valve, which only the most senior operators were allowed to touch and which they turned, only so far, at a critical point in the process. Years later, when the facility was taken apart, workmen found that the valve was no longer connected to anything. It was round and made of metal, but it certainly looked like a horse. Letting such nonuseful animals go—and knowing precisely why—helped make it possible for the company to get its operations fully under control at a time when much of American industry still rode along comfortably on its tacit knowledge.

Things are no different today. Traditional knowledge flourishes in all parts of a company's operations. In the pulp and paper mills studied by Shoshana Zuboff of Harvard Business School,

> one man judged the condition of paper coming off a dry roller by the sensitivity of his hair to electricity in the atmosphere around the machine. Another man could judge the moisture content of a roll of pulp by a quick slap of his hand.

These men are experts at what they do and understand it better than anyone else. Still, as one of the managers put it,

> There are a lot of operators working here who cannot verbally give a description of some piece of the process. I can ask them what is going on at the far end of the plant and they can't tell me but they can draw it for me. By taking away this physical contact that he understands [through computer-based automa-

tion of the process], it's like we have taken away his blueprint. He can't verbalize his way around the process.

Indeed, as one of the engineers told Zuboff,

> There are operators who can run the paper machine with tremendous efficiency, but they cannot describe to you how they do it. . . . One operation required pulling 2 levers simultaneously, and they were not conscious of the fact they were pulling 2 levers. They said they were pulling one. The operators run the mill, but they don't understand how. There are operators who know exactly what to do, but they cannot tell you how they do it.[50]

The fact that such hands-on knowledge is often tacit makes it difficult, of course, to automate operations. Slapping a roll of pulp to judge its moisture content is worlds apart from monitoring items on a computer screen. It is not just a slightly different way of doing the same thing. Those who study the effects of automation on work and workers are deeply concerned with precisely these differences. Where will the strongest resistance to change come from? they wonder. What in traditional practice will be most difficult to overturn?

These are legitimate concerns in both factory and office. White-collar work is hardly immune. Think, for example, of the strides being finally made in getting the expertise and wisdom of professionals like lawyers, accountants, and technologists codified in artificial intelligence programs. Left uncodified, such gut-feel knowledge and instinctive rules of thumb change very closely. Yes, they will adapt, but their center of gravity will not budge easily.

Left to its own devices, all tradition—and the tacit knowledge that supports it—will turn resistance to change into a high form of art. If, however, we are forced to make all such knowledge explicit and hold it up against the demands of present circumstance, we cannot help but see in the starkest terms where we must let go. Or so runs a familiar argument. Show us that the valve on the wall is not attached to anything, and we will readily give up the knee-jerk reflex with which we turn it. Give us statistical evidence of variation amongst different batches of soap, and we will throw open the curtain of secrecy and stick to the formula cards.

Fat chance. We may well set loose a horse, give up a valve, and take down a curtain. But we will not do so with a glad heart and a polite bow. Odds are, we will fight like hell, kick like a mule, and scream bloody murder. In the end, though, we will give up or amend that portion of our tradition which defines the approaches we take to practical ends. We *will* ultimately, if not happily, bow to utility. Remember, the tradition we follow both does something and says something. It is partly instrumental and partly for show. What makes it so hard for us to give any of it up is that we are no better able than soap makers or pulp-machine operators to tell which part is which, even when we try to. It is terribly difficult to separate out the doing from the saying, to distinguish what we must keep, for a while anyway, and what we can with impunity let go.

This distinction between doing and saying, between utility and symbolism, is not a matter fit only for the attention of absentminded philosophers on their more ethereal days. It has immediate cash value. Getting the distinction right tells us which things in our inherited past we may have some control over in the present, and which not. It begins to make that past usable. Consider a specialty merchandiser like L. L. Bean, which has carefully applied modern technology to its order processing and distribution systems without losing its down-home image as a reliable, old-fashioned provider of Maine-style outdoor goods. Using telecommunications and automated warehouses is not, these days, all that hard to do. Using them in the service of a well-established, traditional identity is. Bean's accomplishment is not that it went high-tech. Not at all. It found a way to make its past usable while adjusting to current business needs. That is where the real achievement lies.

If, in a moment of irritation, we want to have done with such refinements and blow the whole kit and caboodle of tradition to smithereens, we ought pause to remember what we stand to lose. Yes, we can detonate horse, valve, and curtain, but in doing so we give up as well much of what holds us loyal and committed in place. Or we can try to prevent the tethering of horse, valve and curtain to begin with. But then we sacrifice all that having them near to hand allows us to do and be—and show.

This, too, is a critical reminder. In our muddleheadedness, we often think that we would be much better off

without tradition, without inherited things that we do or
show, that accomplish work or symbolize something.
Why not do today's job only with today's implements? A
fair question. But there is an answer: As the makers of
New Coke have discovered, today's tools simply do not
enjoy the ready power of self-legitimation, of enlisting
commitment and allegiance, so richly possessed by traditional implements. Yes, new-built creations can grow
to move us or hold us, sometimes quickly. And, yes,
things well established can quickly lose their power. As
a veteran commentator from the CBS News Department
wrote in the wake of the most recent management up-
heavals at the parent company, "CBS does not stand for
anything any more. They are just corporate initials now."
Still, traditional arrangements do possess a special force
that can have a great practical value—if managed well.

The issue, then, is twofold: first, to make a judicious
discrimination between the parts of our tradition that are
for doing and for show; and second, to displace, as best
we can, the emotions attached to the useful parts onto
objects more properly suited to current needs and circumstances. (At the outset, what is there only for show
we had best leave pretty much alone, for it is the source
of the emotion we need. To rip it loose from its moorings
by force will likely trigger an explosion or an inner collapse that we ought be eager to avoid.) The displacement
of such emotion, however, is something that we can—
and should—seek. We *can* ennoble the present with
energies generated through our traditional attachments.
In fact, that may well be the only sustainable way to do

so. Fresh-made cultures like those of so many high-tech start-ups do not hold together, do not have much staying power, do not generate any lasting call on our allegiance. In fact, as current studies of new venture success confirm, the ventures that do well usually have a management team that worked together for some time in the past. We truly give of ourselves in the present only when our deeper commitments have been enlisted—that is, only when there has been careful management of the displacement of tradition.

The Process of Displacement

It *is* possible through displacement—through the careful attachment of venerable emotions to new objects—to define the past that defines our present. If we prove able to distinguish utility from symbolism, we *can* make a selection from among all the stuff in the great storehouse of tradition. We, too, can create a world with ancient fossils already embedded in it. Consider, for example, one of the greatest of all such accomplishments in this line: the deliberate fabrication begun in the eighteenth century for political ends of the so-called Highland Tradition in Scotland, a collection of cultural odds and ends that was supposed to have been in existence from time immemorial. All the now familiar trappings—kilts, bagpipes, tartan cloth woven in distinctive patterns for each clan, epic poetry heralding the deeds of noble past heroes—were parts of this invention. To be sure, there had been hints of some of this earlier, but the framing concept of a united cultural tradition, long and distinguished, was an intentional creation of the eighteenth and nineteenth centuries.

According to the historian Hugh Trevor-Roper,

> The creation of an independent Highland tradition, and the imposition of that new tradition, with its outward badges, on the whole Scottish nation, was the work of the later eighteenth and early nineteenth centuries. It occurred in three stages. First, there was the cultural revolt against Ireland: the usurpation of Irish culture and the re-writing of early Scottish history, culminating in the insolent claim that Scotland—Celtic Scotland—was the 'mother-nation' and Ireland the cultural dependency. Second, there was the artificial creation of new Highland traditions, presented as ancient, original and distinctive. Thirdly, there was the process by which these new traditions were offered to, and adopted by, historical Lowland Scotland: the Eastern Scotland of the Picts, the Saxons, and the Normans.[51]

Before the Union with England, the apparatus of this tradition, to the extent it existed at all, was—and was by other Scots regarded as being—the trappings of a barbarous, roguish, and backward people, who were themselves a broken and scattered fragment of Irish culture. The great literature of the tradition, ostensibly discovered and translated during the 1760s, was an out-and-out forgery. The essential costume—the modern small kilt— was introduced to the Highlands in the late 1720s by an English Quaker, Thomas Rawlinson. Rawlinson thought it would make a more practical working garb for the local employees of his iron-smelting operation than the voluminous belted plaid they were accustomed to. Only after the rebellion of 1745, when the British tried to stamp out Highland resistance by outlawing its costume and deposing the chiefs of its clans, only then did the middle and upper classes adopt the fashion in private as a badge of identity and self-definition.

There is a bit more to the story. According to Trevor-Roper, when the ban was finally lifted,

> the fashion spread. Anglicized Scottish peers, improving gentry, well-educated Edinburgh lawyers and prudent merchants of Aberdeen—men who were not constrained by poverty and who would never have to skip over rocks and bogs or lie all night in the hills—would exhibit themselves publicly not in the historic trews [trousers], the traditional costume of their class . . . but in a costly and fanciful version of that recent innovation, the philibeg or small kilt.[52]

Nor were clan-to-clan differences in tartan plaid an ancient custom. Highland regiments, allowed to wear the kilt for its convenience after 1725, chose different patterns as a visible way of quickly differentiating themselves. The extension of these differences to civilian wearers did not become widespread until 1819, when William Wilson and Son of Bannockburn, manufacturers, entered into an alliance with the Highland Society of London, itself a creation of 1778, to certify the varieties in its "Key Pattern Book" as ancient possessions of this or that clan. It was a brilliant commercial strategy to segment the market and boost demand.

And where did the impulse to assign—as if by ancient

right—off-the-peg pattern number 155 to Cluny
MacPherson come from? In 1819 plans first surfaced for
a state visit to Edinburgh three years later by George IV.
Sir Walter Scott, he of the mighty pen, urged the clan
chiefs to come pay homage to the king decked out in all
their "traditional" finery. The manufacturers were only
too glad to oblige.

So it was that political resistance, cultural inferiority,
military necessity, process engineering, social mobility,
status anxiety, and commercial demand-side management all combined to create a new ancient tradition. It is
a marvelous tale, true in its details, and not at all unusual. We may be tempted to smile at the pretensions of
these Scots or their gullibility, but we ought to think
twice. As any followers of Ralph Lauren's Polo collection
should understand, the fabrication of the Highland tradition through displacement rises above the commonplace only because it was so very successful and on such
a broad scale.

The instrumental quality of these Highland trappings
and appointments assured their acceptance as soon as
their benefits could be demonstrated. Not without a
struggle, perhaps, but sooner rather than later. What
held them in place, however, what gave them a call on
emotion and loyalty, what rooted them in experience—
in short, what fixed them in daily routines was not what
they did but what they said. A clever Bannockburn manufacturer may have wished to keep his looms busy by
getting the Scots to outfit themselves in this or that pattern. But if they went along with his ploy, they did so not

to boost his ROI or to keep themselves covered. They wished to do something practical, and his material gave them the means—through displacement.

Within limits, then, it is possible to make the past usable or, at need, to create a past that is usable. In each case, the managerial task is much like Edmund Burke's classic program for conservatism: to change in order to conserve. In institutional terms, this means to displace the emotional commitments of tradition onto new objects and arrangements. We want to be proud of our store-bought Highland costume.

One way or another, by intent or by accident, such displacement goes on all the time. By the late 1950s, for example, Alcoa Laboratories, which had long focused on cutting-edge research in metallurgy and electrochemistry, had turned its attention to shorter-term, engineering-oriented issues. Enhanced domestic competition and an assumption that the company's well of technical knowledge was filled high enough to serve for years made this switch in emphasis plausible. By the mid-1980s, however, Alcoa had lost much of its ability to do cutting-edge work. In particular, it had to write off some two decades of effort trying to develop a major new smelting process. As the best available study of the situation puts it, "The magnitude of the failure reflected attempts to pursue long-term revolutionary goals in a short-term incremental environment." Self-image had not kept up with changed circumstances.

Peter Bridenbaugh, Alcoa's vice president for research, came to see that "insights into past changes in

Alcoa's conception of what its research and development laboratory should be [would give] us a crucial perspective on and understanding of the roots of our current problems. . . . I began to appreciate the penalty we were paying for changes that had occurred in the years following the war."[53] In other words, a close look at how the Laboratories' mission had evolved over time made visible the process of displacement. Outdated assumptions of fundamental technical expertise had attached themselves to a more limited kind of technical effort. But a new adjustment of management policies could in fact nurture the kind of expertise long assumed to exist.

Displacements of the latter sort are not easy to accomplish, but they are surely possible. First, though, we must understand just how it is that, willy-nilly, we redefine our relation to the past all the time. The activity of displacement, as we are talking about it here, is part of a larger adaptive process that is always in motion. It is a special instance of a general circumstance. The past, for us, is not a fixed and immutable thing but is continuously in the process of becoming what we next know it to be.

We often underestimate, and underestimate badly, how gradual things are, preferring to think about them as if they represented simply points in times. Processes of slow, adaptive change are all about us. In the corporate world, for example, decisions do not get made or implemented all of a sudden. They have a certain duration. What we remember long after the fact as a crisp determination to expand a product line or make the fellow down the block an offer he cannot refuse was, at the time, merely the tip of a rather large iceberg. Both line expansion and gentle offer grow out of thought, study, and discussion, much of which takes place out of sight. Even if a CEO pounds a fist upon the table in memorable fashion and says, "Let's do it—now!" that timber-rattling order does not emerge from a vacuum. All was not dark and void a day or a week or a month before. More likely than not, parts of what become an idea or a decision churn around in solution for some length of time before getting precipitated out in the form of a hard crystal of fact.

Our language plays us false by causing us to think that the stuff out of which the past is composed is neatly organized in separate little boxes, about which we can entertain discrete—and fixed—opinions. We talk as if decisions were things that do not exist one moment but are there, in all their solidity, the next. We talk the same way about innovations and discoveries. If we believe the language of our schoolbooks, Joseph Priestley—and Priestley alone—discovered oxygen at a single moment in time. Abracadabra. Well, that is simply not the way it was. Nor did Alfred Sloan at GM see his way to segment the automobile market at a single instant, before which his thoughts and researches never touched upon the problem. Or what about that great inventor, Edison, and the electric light? At which point in his ceaseless experimentation do we point a finger and say, That's when it happened? For convenience, we would have things be simpler than they are, which is fair enough and perfectly understandable. But it is also misleading.

Even the crispest and most abrupt decisions have duration, a certain extension in time. In his *My Forty Years with Ford*, Charles Sorensen recollects that Henry Ford himself

> had no ideas on mass production. He wanted to build a lot of autos. He was determined but, like everyone else at that time, he didn't know how. In later years he was glorified as the originator of the mass production idea. Far from it; he just grew into it, like the rest of us. The essential tools and the final assembly line with its many integrated feeders resulted from an organization which was continually experimenting and improvising to get better production.[54]

By contrast, the popular belief, only slightly exaggerated, is that Ford hit upon the idea for his mass production system out of the blue and then spent the necessary time and resources to implement it. Not so. Like Priestley, Sloan, Edison—like all of us—Ford was leaning in a particular direction, trying this and that to move a bit further along, making adjustments here and there as he went. His accomplishment, which we commonly discuss as if it happened at a stroke, did no such thing. It slowly unfolded in time. But we tend to remember the fact and forget the process. We fail to recognize the incremental nature of much that we prefer to remember as a single bold stroke. The failure matters because incrementalism of this sort allows room for management, for the careful direction of change.

"Gunfire at Sea," Elting Morison's justly famous study of the introduction of continuous-air firing in the United States Navy, makes much of the resistance against which this excellent innovation had to struggle. Vested interests arrayed themselves against it. Men who should have known better either refused to believe or tried to discredit the facts of its superior performance. These were not evil men trying to work harm. Not at all. Instead, they were, as Morison describes them, "victims of *severely limited* identifications"—that is, they were profoundly attached, in thought and sentiment, to existing technology and the social customs that surrounded it. They were comfortable with their world as it was and hostile to anything that might seriously disrupt it. At some level, they recognized how deeply the current technology was bound up with the apparatus of a particular social order, an order with which they were deeply identified. And they were right. Continuous firing would change their world.

Had these men been wiser and more flexible, they would not have seen the alternative to their resistance as scrapping everything about the Navy as they knew it so as to start over with a clean slate. Neither blind resistance to change nor wholesale junking of the past makes for sensible development. Gradual adaptation does. Decisions, discoveries, and innovations are not brilliant flashes of the knife, which sunder what follows from all that went before. In themselves—and especially in the institutional contexts through which they work—they represent *processes* of change, gradual unfoldings, piece-by-piece rearrangements of prior identifications and allegiances. They represent an on-going adaptation to the ever-shifting mix of what past and present make available. Displacement goes on, in a sense, all the time.

This, too, is the lesson Morison draws: The institutions that survive and prosper are adaptive in that they "select judiciously from the ideas and material presented both by the past and present and . . . throw them into a new combination." They neither abandon their traditions nor cleave to them with blind obedience. They muddle along with a "kind of resilience that . . . enable[s] [them] to accept fully and easily the best promises of changing circumstances without losing [their] sense of continuity or . . . essential integrity." In other words, like Alcoa's R&D operation, they change in order to conserve.[55]

Adaptation by muddling along does not imply a necessarily accidental or random or incoherent process. It does not mean that we cannot or should not plan, direct, and order. Least of all does it mean that we must sacrifice at one stroke who we most deeply are or the continuity with our past that tradition provides. All it means is that our traditions, rightly understood, continuously demand of us not rigid observance but gradual and incremental redefinition.

Anyone who has ever watched a corporate unit fall upon hard times knows full well how easy it is to destroy the cohesion and integrity that it took years to build.

There is no trick to freeing things up by the careful placement of explosives. The hard work of management is not
to enforce change by calling in air support to drop a few
big ones behind our own lines. Any idiot can do that. No,
the real challenge is to guide the awkward, sloppy, uneven, and unending process of gradual adaptation to shifting circumstance—and to do so without brokering or
blowing away the sense of continuity that tells us who we
are. IBM today is not exactly as it was a generation ago,
yet no one would doubt that it is the same company, that
what has made it special in mainframes is what has allowed
it to do so well with personal computers.

We make a serious error when we think of our traditions, the stuff of our continuity, as completed things
that require defense and maintenance only. Our past is
not finished, eternally set, unable to be shaped. Like a
coral reef, traditions are always in process, always alive,
always changing. The work of building them is never
over. They are never complete. Who would argue that
the Catholic Church or the institution of the papacy,
those archetypes of tradition in the modern world, are
just as they were a century or a millennium ago? Who
would want them to be? And who would want them to be
present-minded creatures of fashion that shifted their
values and beliefs and ceremonies to accommodate each
flutter of popular opinion? Institutions that remain vital
over time know how to live *in* time, know how to possess
the past by gradually redefining their own relation to it.
What they—and we—possess through tradition is something that we and they can help shape.

Tradition consists, we must remember, in both a mode of knowing and a particular body of things known. When we talk about our partial ability to shape it and to have a hand in defining our own relevant past, we do not imply that we have some privileged access to a time machine. We cannot finesse *how* we know things. Nor is there any way we can go back in time to that April evening at Ford's Theater and steer John Wilkes Booth away from a certain private box. All we mean is that we do have some freedom to select the useful pieces from the much larger collection of all that we are and have been. This is what Auden meant when he referred to our modern "consciousness of the whole of the past in the present." Making the past usable is not an exercise like that of making up pre-Soviet history out of whole cloth in a contemporary Moscow university. It is, rather, a more limited process of reinterpretation, the exercise of a new principle of selection. We amend our Constitution, not worship or abandon it.

II

Here, then, is a most effective lever for managing change: the choice of relevant but unused portions of tradition and the gradual attachment to them of emotions originally attached elsewhere. With care, the pieces of an apparently seamless tradition *do* come apart. It *is* possible to separate what is there for utility from what is there for show or statement. And it *is* possible to cover novel practical arrangements with the attitudes and emotions

generated by pieces that are ostensibly "useless"—the
furled umbrellas, hard hats, powdered wigs, and cavalry
spurs. This is, after all, precisely what displacement
means: the gradual, step-by-step rearrangement of prior
identifications and allegiances.

In many an attic somewhere, there is a large steamer
trunk filled with all sorts of practical odds and ends. We
can, to some degree, dip into it at need. We can even
slip in something new once in a while. When we are
done with a particular item, back into the trunk it goes,
forgotten perhaps but not lost. It may stay there in ob-
scurity for years. Out of sight and out of mind. But it
does not disappear. It does not evaporate. With effort,
we can find it again on purpose or even stumble over it
by accident. Tradition works the same way that trunk
does. It holds far more than we use—or are even aware
of—at any one time. It has the potential for supplying us
with more combinations and permutations of things than
we can readily imagine. The steamer trunk of tradition
exists and is available to us—if only we know it.

This is why it is so important to remember the "built"
quality of our world, the fact that we live in Troy surrounded by hitches. This is why it is so important to view
decisions and judgments and discoveries not as sudden,
hard nuggets of fact but as composite items with duration
and density, as things built up out of shreds and patches
over time. We need to remember that our trunk holds
other things still and that our current selections are just
that—selections. We could choose otherwise, make other
selections.

The anthropologist Claude Lévi-Strauss describes the primitive mind as working the way a *bricoleur* or handyman does. It has a sizable but finite kit bag of tools to deploy when confronted with the shifting tasks and challenges of life. *Bricolage*, the work of tool selection and rearrangement, is much the same thing we do when we use our alphabet or sit down in front of a piano or try to manage our traditions. We draw upon a finite set of elements and use them to create a seemingly infinite range of responses. But we can do so only if we remember that the ways in which we usually pick and combine these elements are not the only ways in which they can be picked or combined. Our familiar structures are just that—familiar—not inevitable. They are constructs. They could have been otherwise. They could have taken other forms. Hours need not be equal in length. We could have conceptualized the videodisc project in different ways. With our steamer trunk in the attic, we are *bricoleurs* of tradition. And if we make new choices, we can through displacements fill them with a sense of legitimacy and wrap them in our commitment.

At least, the possibility exists. Confronted by deregulation and the divestiture of its local operating companies, AT&T could not continue to manage itself as the comfortable monopoly it had long been. Both within and without the company, the question was asked, Can they change their stripes? Can they fight for a market? Can they play the new product development game in a universe where product generations get measured in months not decades? Can they harness their world-class basic research more directly to their current operational needs? Like it or not, the business press piously intoned, AT&T would have to try to make itself over. The implication in all this, of course, was that company history was relevant here only as a barrier, an obstacle, as something to be overcome and then forcibly disavowed. Tradition for Ma Bell meant complacency and sluggishness within the protective and often stultifying embrace of Uncle Sam—nothing more and nothing less.

Hogwash. AT&T has not always been a lumbering giant in a slow growth industry with standardized technology and negligible competition. It has not always stood in the midst of the financial ocean like a massive rock of Gibraltar, the common stock of preference for widows, orphans, and conservative portfolios. It has not always rested securely on a technical base that could ignore with impunity advances on other fronts and in other laboratories. As we have seen, AT&T was once an upstart operation in an industry with no certain definition, no clear market structure, no assured pattern of competition, no confident understanding of how it might best participate in the nation's emerging communications nexus, and no reason to be confident that it could find legal ways to protect its distinctive skills from imitators. Amid these uncertainties and more, the company scrambled, fought, experimented, and won.

Is it meaningful, then, to view AT&T's steamer trunk as the repository of smug complacency and nothing else? Does it make sense to think of the company as having no vital connection with anything in its past that might bear upon the chaotic world of deregulated competition? Is it legitimate to treat Ma Bell's complex, multifaceted tradition as if it contained but a single strain of experience—and that of recent vintage? Of course not. Now, this does not mean that AT&T can simply dip back into its early past and pull out of its trunk a few handy pieces that speak directly to the problems that currently lie before it. But it does mean that, to address those problems, AT&T does not have to become something it never was. It needs, instead, to recapture something of what it used to be—to focus, for example, on the rapid commercialization of new technology, on the replacement of outdated transmission and switching equipment, and on the services with which it can compete against other entrants in specific markets.

This difference might not sound like much, a bit of verbal juggling only. But the gaping abyss between radical transformation and renaissance is wide enough to drive a whole industry through with room to spare. Radical, root-and-branch change has few institutional resources on which to call for support. It must carry its own legitimacy and staying power with it. By contrast, change—even quite major change—that works by recapturing something that was there in the past has many resources on which to draw and a whole network of support on which to rely. Label a new law as constitutional, and the whole elaborate apparatus of sanctioned legitimacy springs into action to embrace it. Argue, however, for the establishment of a monarchical system of government, and the silence will be deafening.

When, as with AT&T, present upheaval requires of a company not a new approach built from scratch but some new principle of connection with forgotten strands in its own history, the graft is much more likely to take—and to flourish. The ideal of universal telephone service need not mean a civil service view of the world. In one particular set of circumstances it may have come to mean that, but it does not have to. Universal service is not incompatible with scrappy, competitive behavior, and both are part of AT&T's heritage.

When current need prompts a different selection from among the items in our steamer trunk, the mere fact that they come—and can be known to come—from *our* trunk does much to avoid normal problems of organizational rejection. In fact, the institutional memory which that trunk holds serves not so much as a barrier to change but as a kind of facilitating or enabling agent of change. The very act of rummaging about and making a new selection, one geared to altered circumstances, is the central means by which the purposeful displacement of tradition gets accomplished. It is how we redefine our relation to the past in such a way as to make the past usable. And it is how we can elicit the genuine commitment of our people to whatever new direction we choose to take. Items from the trunk have an immediate call on our in-built mechanisms of allegiance, loyalty, and support.

A few years back, Sears faced shrinking margins in its retail business, low growth prospects even where margins held, and a change in urban demography and buying patterns that threatened its long-established network of retail stores. The suburban shopping malls, which we now take utterly for granted, specialty boutiques, and the economic decay of inner cities had changed the face of the commercial world those stores were designed to serve. What could Sears do? Did it have to write off a century of marketing experience and seek elsewhere for the answers to its present difficulties? Did it have to look at itself honestly and say, Sorry, folks, all we really know how to do is sell goods out of the kinds of stores in the kinds of locations that no longer seem to appeal to you? Did it have to fold up its tent, like the old Baltimore Colts, and steal away under cover of night—if, that is, it could find a way to "fold up" an operation so large? Had it nothing to draw on?

Of course it did. Sears had not been born as a lumbering retail elephant serving blighted urban areas but as an aggressive and imaginative mail-order house serving a rural population mostly of farmers and their families. The move to establish retail stores did not come easily. In its time, it was a great revolution, a scary and dangerous move. The man who made it happen, General Robert E. Wood, had had the idea for years. It first came to him, so the story goes, while he was chief quartermaster to George W. Goethals during the building of the Panama Canal. To while away his free hours in Panama, Wood turned to the pages of the *Statistical Abstract of the United States,* an odd source of entertainment, perhaps, but not for Wood, whose work on the Canal project—and later in the army during World War I— involved the mastery of supply management (in the army he was to be general merchandise manager). After the war, in his new position at the mail-order house of Montgomery Ward, Wood tried to urge the results of his studies on Ward's management. They were unmoved.

And what was the gist of Wood's unwelcome message? Simply this: A close reading of the demographic evidence showed that the United States was rapidly losing its rural character and becoming an urban nation. In addition, Henry Ford's success in mass-producing automobiles made it possible for farm families to drive into town on occasion and do the kind of shopping in person that they used to do only through the mail. As a result, Ward had better think about using its strengths in distribution, purchasing, and reputation to establish a retail operation. This, it soon became clear to Wood, the top people at Ward did not want to do.

At Sears, the reaction was different. Julius Rosenwald hired Wood as vice-president in charge of factories and retail stores and four years later made him president of the entire company, even though that meant losing several other top managers with long and valuable experience in the company. Success in the new retailing venture did not come quickly or painlessly, but Wood and Rosenwald remained convinced that they were on the right course. As Wood himself noted, business is like war. If its grand strategy is correct, any number of tactical errors can be made and yet the basic enterprise proves successful. With a deep conviction of the appropriateness of its grand strategy, Sears learned as it went. Only gradually did it build itself into the retailing dinosaur that a later generation would regard as having been a permanent fixture on the commercial landscape since the moment when Adam and Eve first had to worry about dry goods.

The point in retelling this story is not to rehearse again the merits of Wood's vision or Rosenwald's courage. It is to underscore a plain but often overlooked fact about the stuff that sits in the steamer trunk at Sears. In the company's inventory of tradition, in the collections of its past upon which it can draw at need, there is more than the experience of being a lumbering retail giant. As with AT&T, that trunk holds a fairly wide variety of items, many of which speak directly to a time when things were fragile and uncertain, success was far from assured, and every new step was heavily freighted with risk. In retrospect, the movement into store-based retailing seems obvious and inevitable. At the time, it was a bold gamble—a gamble based on solid evidence and analysis, to be sure, but no less a throw of the dice for that. We err greatly when we read later certainty back into earlier moments of choice. Not only do we get the nature and quality of that earlier decision wrong. More important, we ignore and discredit important parts of who we are. The impulse, the reflex, is to identify our traditions only with the content of our major accomplishments. This is a huge error. Without a qualm we assert that Ma Bell knows how to be a comfortable monopoly, and Sears knows how to be a retail merchant. Yes, these are things both companies know about and have done, but they do not represent all that these companies are or know. In both cases, the steamer trunk holds more than last week's or last month's garment. In fact, the relevant tradition for each is not just this or that particular accomplishment but the demonstrated ability to adapt and adjust to changing circumstances.

For the most part, we think of tradition as embodying substance (mastery of retail selling, mastery of regulated telephone service), not process (the ability to adapt and change). No one doubts that substance is important. Experience in running a fish market does not easily translate into the expertise needed to build petrochemical plants. But process is important, too—especially given our tendency to dwell on content only. There was a time that both AT&T and Sears had to scramble, amidst a chorus of doubters and nay-sayers and in the face of conventional wisdom, to find the path with which we now so calmly and completely identify them. We remember that path easily enough, but we forget the scrambling.

Challenged by Japanese producers and shifting market preferences, General Motors has had to rethink its manufacturing process and its organizational structure. In a company so large and capital-intensive, change of this magnitude is terribly expensive and disruptive. There is great reluctance to face up to it, to let the arrangements of the "good old days" during, say, the 1950s slip away. Managers who have grown up within so elaborate and successful an institutional context are understandably reluctant to pull it apart brick by brick. In their dreams float visions of building new V-8 gas guzzlers with big profit margins that a car-happy public cannot get enough of. All this is perfectly understandable and predictable. It is hard to turn an aircraft carrier at full steam around on a dime. As anyone not asleep for the past dozen years can attest, the magnitude of the challenge has not been a mystery. GM has had its hands full.

In this battle—and battle it is—both press and management have usually treated the company's tradition as a great impediment to the task at hand. How is it possible, runs the common question, to disassemble the house that Sloan built? Once again, this is the wrong question. Alfred P. Sloan, during his many years at the top of GM, did indeed build a complex structure to hold the far-flung activities of the corporation together in a sensible and productive fashion. But he did not build it all at once at the outset of his tenure and then simply fill in nearly invisible chinks from time to time.

What Sloan created was a skeleton that he and his people modified at need, as circumstances changed and as they amassed a better understanding of the challenges that faced them. The relevant tradition here is not defined by the cumbersome apparatus in place when the first Toyotas landed on American docks. It is not the content of any particular organizational set. It is, rather, the company's long history of imaginative uses of structure to adapt to the world about it. There is a legitimate tradition of process here, of experimentation and adjustment, of continuous displacement, not simply of rigid V-8-dom.

GM's recent realignment of its automotive divisions into two major groups is, then, nothing new. Certainly, it represents a substantial change in organization, but the salient fact is that such changes are themselves nothing new. The ability to make them, to view them as experiments, to treat them in the normal course of events as subject to modification over time—this, too, sits in the steamer trunk in GM's attic. As still more recent events have shown, however, the inertia against which such rummaging in the attic must push can often be paralyzing. The much-vaunted Saturn project has lost most of its status as radical experiment, and EDS has been captured by the dead weight of GM culture. There is, in practice, nothing to prevent managers from grabbing onto the wrong things in the attic. As Roger Smith notes, "We have guys who say, 'Hey, we came through this recession and that recession, we survived the oil shocks, we turned a $760-million loss a few years ago into a $4-billion profit. Why would anybody want to come in here and tell us to do anything differently *now*?' "[56]

Even so, the point worth remembering is that many of the right things or, at least, of the more useful things are waiting up there to be discovered too. For all GM's backsliding, it still possesses a tradition of radical experimentation that can be tapped at need. To move forward, it need not undertake a wholesale abandonment of tradition but rather, a careful selection of which strands of available tradition to emphasize and build upon. The task is not to deny or amputate the past but to identify and embrace those parts of it that are now relevant.

In the world of consumer goods, Procter & Gamble has long enjoyed a much-deserved reputation as a juggernaut of marketing skills. Its mastery of research and testing, of advertising, and of trade policies is the stuff of which business school textbooks speak with approval. But when, of late, its dominance in traditional product lines began to wane and its investment in new product development depressed current earnings, loud keening could be heard for the passing of a once-mighty giant. And again, behind the keening, could also be heard the familiar question: How can tradition-bound P&G, with its rule book of procedures and policies, hope to meet the new competitive realities facing it? And again, this was the wrong question.

Did the trunk in that Cincinnati attic contain a single rule book and nothing more? Balderdash. Years ago, when middlemen and speculators made demand for the company's product irregular although their use by consumers was steady and predictable, P&G made the bold decision to bypass those middlemen entirely and sell directly to retailers. At the time, it was not at all clear whether the policy would stick or whether it would destroy the company. In the ever-accurate business press, the initials P&G rapidly came to mean "passed and gone." But as Mark Twain gleefully observed on a similar occasion, rumors of its death were greatly exaggerated. And when, on another occasion, other brands of soap than Ivory failed to receive the marketing support they needed, P&G took the equally unprecedented step of throwing its own brands into competition with each other. And when, after World War II, the long development work on synthetic detergents led to the creation of Tide, this supposedly stodgy company, mired in its bog of traditional practice, moved immediately to full-scale production without taking the usual step of first building a pilot plant.

What, then, is the real P&G tradition: a commitment to a specific body of deliberate, systematic practice or a willingness to take on substantial risk when the situation merits? This is what sophomores ask. Juniors and seniors ought to recognize that the company's tradition embodies both these strains—and more besides. There is far more in that trunk than readily meets the eye. At each juncture, the issue for management is which piece or pieces to focus on, which to emphasize, which to embrace as relevant, which to build upon. As with AT&T, Sears, and GM, the challenge for P&G is not to become something it never was but to recapture part of what it used to be and has been all along.

These are all familiar stories, intentionally so. The purpose of retelling them here is to cast a slightly different light on what we think we already know. Behind and beneath the quite different substance of these accomplishments lies an identifiable pattern of response.

But it is a pattern of the sort we have a hard time recognizing. It speaks not to strategic choice, though choice is involved. Nor to particular structural arrangements, though organizational changes matter. Nor to specific functional policies, though such policies are central. It speaks, rather, to a certain quality of experience, a certain hospitality to the richness and variety of what these companies have been and done in the past. It speaks to an ability—and a willingness—to manage the displacement of tradition. It enlarges our sense of what the professional manager's job entails. It identifies a resource for effecting change that we are otherwise all too ready to ignore. Or have already forgotten.

It is odd, given the current fascination with issues of leadership, how little attention gets paid to the ability of true leaders to release the creative energies of their people by putting them in touch with relevant, if forgotten, aspects of their shared past. We may have grown comfortable in our urban occupations, but when a young Democratic president calls us to a "new frontier," we feel the pull of a past that we never knew directly—but that is no less ours, today, because our possession comes only through recollected tradition.

In December 1981, Motorola announced that it was going to buy Four-Phase Systems, Inc., a maker of computers, for a quarter billion dollars. The doubters had a field day, pushing down the value of Motorola stock by 10 percent in a single week. This was a new technical area for the company, a new business. Why should anyone think that a company with so spotty an acquisitions record would get it right this time around? What reason was there to believe Motorola could successfully take on something so different from what it knew how to do?

Several decades before, in the mid-1950s, the company had faced an important decision about its relatively small transistor operations. Either it had to scale them up in significant fashion or get out. Paul Galvin and many of his top managers leaned toward getting out. What they were comfortable with was equipment manufacturing, not cutting-edge advances in electronics. Moving into transistors in a big way and, beyond that, into semiconductors also meant trying to enlist as customers outside companies with which Motorola often competed for the sale of equipment. This was unfamiliar, tricky ground. But the importance of staying on top of this new technology was too great, finally, to ignore. The company plunged in—with, as it turned out, happy results.

This earlier experience does not suggest that any new departure, like the acquisition of Four-Phase Systems, is a good thing no matter how initially disruptive. Nor does it suggest that competent execution of such plans is inevitable. Hardly. All it suggests is that when the company thinks through in the future who it is and what it can do, the answer should reflect an awareness of all that it has been, not just part. No one can go back and make things in the past turn out differently than they have. But it is possible to select, to choose among, items in the steamer trunk and to determine which of them are now to be seen as relevant, to be used as a basis for action, to serve as a rallying point for commitment.

Learning How to Remember

Making the past usable does not mean rewriting it. All it means is identifying what is presently relevant in the collection of traditional odds and ends. The mechanics of such displacement permit, at times, stunning degrees of change and reorientation. They allow an automaker like GM to follow a technology-driven course with the EDS and Hughes acquisitions. They do not restrict us to modest, nearly invisible alterations. They do not condemn us to a measure of novelty visible only under a microscope. What they do, instead, is to provide the unbroken, incremental, step-by-step process of transition by which we get from here to there. To rummage about and make new selections is not to deny who we are but to rediscover all we have been. And this kind of rediscovery— the intentional choice of a relevant past—need not cut us off from what holds us together as a functioning social group or institution. It is, in an important sense, a process of return, not a process of abandonment. But it is not a process of return that we can always undertake at once. Quite often, we can take possession only gradually, only so fast as our fears or inhibitions or reluctances allow us.

During the early years of the American nation, for example, Benjamin Franklin's autobiography, the last pieces of which were finished just before his death in 1790, was known to the American public, if at all, only through editions put together abroad. That situation did

not change until 1818. Why? True, the publishing history of the document is unusually complex. Even so,
Franklin's grandson, who brought out the 1818 edition,
explained the delay by noting "there are *times* and *seasons* when prudence imposes the restriction of silence in
the gratification of even the most laudable curiosity."[57]
There was a conscious decision to wait. Again, why?

We will probably never know for sure. One likely
explanation, however, is that the great convulsions in
Europe precipitated by the French Revolution and the
career of Napoleon did not create the sort of environment in which a domestic edition of the autobiography
could comfortably sally forth. In a new and still quite
fragile nation, the specter of a self-made man "from the
provinces" shouldering his way into prominence and
control by his own ambition and clever maneuvering
might reasonably make people a bit uneasy. The raw
edges of a system still insecurely in place do not always
make a happy or a welcome reminder. The less than
polite machinations in the streets of a revolutionary generation quickly fade out of sight, to be replaced by ex-
panding memories of sober "founding fathers" in halls of
well-ordered political debate. Napoleon's career was a
stark reminder of what lay behind that proper and re-
spectable facade. Only when the new system is secure
enough, only when the facade is firmly enough in place,
can we tolerate strong evidence of the chaos behind it.

This is not an isolated example. The western gun-
slinger did not become a character of romantic appeal to

the general public until the social order of western com-
munities was well enough established in fact to make
these shady operators a dying breed. The Indian only
became a figure of primitive nobility in the popular
imagination as native tribes of a region ceased to pose a
serious threat to local whites. The hard-boiled dick of
twentieth-century detective novels did not make his appearance until the social order of urban America stopped
threatening to explode at any moment. The cowboy did
not become a colorful loner in distinctive and widely
imitated clothing until the way of life he represented had
largely passed away. Haight-Ashbury styles did not make
their way into suburban shopping malls until the hippie
phenomenon had lost its validity as well as its overtones
of social threat. Distinctive clan kilts were not popular-
ized until Highlanders' political resistance to the British
crown had been broken. Franklin's autobiography was
not an exception.

Social groups remember what they can—and as they
can. In our own lives, we all do the same thing with
difficult memories and experience. We make our peace
with the items in our attic trunk bit by bit. It is no
different in the corporate world.

More than likely, we cannot use everything in the
trunk all at once even if we know the whole range of
what is there. It often takes time before organizations
can absorb in the present the full recollection of what
they have been or known or done in the past. To be
effective, then, the process of displacement takes time,

and no two organizations are identical in how much time
they take. Or in the most appropriate order in which to
absorb things. Or in the proper tempo for moving the
process along. But what else is new? This is no strange
and unprecedented challenge to managers. It is what
their professional tasks always require of them: the ability to judge what a particular organization can do and
what a particular organization needs. Knowledge of the
steamer trunk's existence merely expands the litany of
resources on which they can call in making their decisions and putting them into effect. Managing the process
of displacement does not require special, exotic skills. It
calls only for the application of entirely familiar skills to
novel ends.

III

With such a trunk patiently waiting for us upstairs, it is
easy to forget that—although it holds a lot we have been
slow to acknowledge—it does not hold everything.
Merely because, somewhere in the past, there was a
successful acquisition, diversification, structural adjustment, or whatever, it does not follow that we can just
turn around and apply those lessons today. As we have
seen, the lure of similitude in whatever form is terribly
seductive but often fatal. Idiosyncratic facts matter. The
nuts-and-bolts details of current problems are not quite
like those of any other situation. We should reason from
context to context, from past to present, only with the

greatest care. Rightly understood, the trunk supplies no
instant remedy. It promises no over-the-counter pana-
cea. It offers no miracle cure. All it does is expand the
range of stuff upon which we can comfortably draw because it is part of who we are. It is our gateway to alternative pasts. How we use them is something else again.

In the best sense, then, our attic collection is an enabling resource, a store chest of relevant pasts upon which
we can draw as time and circumstance require. If we
forget the trunk is there or if we choose to ignore it, it
will still make its presence felt. Invisibly, perhaps, but
effectively it will serve as a powerful constraint upon our
present, tethering us to the odd horse. But if used wisely
and managed well, it can help us respond with vigor and
commitment to novel situations. What the very fact of
the trunk makes clear is that we are not so easily classi-
fied as having this skill only or that experience and no
more. We are—and have been—many things. Our rich
and various patrimony does not disappear merely because we do not fully call upon it at any given moment.
It sits in the attic, waiting.

We may, of course, dip into that attic collection for
something as simple as a faded sepia photograph of the
old storefront in order to give a new marketing effort a
strong visual symbol. Our need may be for ornament,
nothing more, and in the collection upstairs there is ornament aplenty. But there is much more, too—if we but
permit ourselves to acknowledge its presence. No pad-
lock bars us from any portion of our copious heritage. No
armed guard turns us back from the continuous redis-

covery of who we are and what we can do. No barrier prevents our gradual, purposeful displacement of tradition. If we keep away, avert our eyes, or stay our hand, the responsibility is ours alone. We *can* make the past usable—if only we will.

Notes

1. Walter Lippmann, *Public Opinion,* reprint ed. (New York: Free Press, 1965), p. 16.
2. Richard Hamermesh, "Making Planning Strategic," *Harvard Business Review,* July–August 1986, p. 117.
3. Robert H. Hayes and Kim B. Clark, "Why Some Factories Are More Productive Than Others," *Harvard Business Review,* September–October 1986.
4. Frederick W. Gluck, "Taking the Mystique out of Planning," *Across the Board,* July–August 1985, p. 57.
5. David S. Landes, *Revolution in Time: Clocks and the Making of the Modern World* (Cambridge, Mass.: Harvard University Press, 1983), p. 33.
6. Daniel J. Boorstin, *The Discoverers: A History of Man's Search to Know His World and Himself* (New York: Random House, 1983), p. 42.
7. Robert H. Krieble, "Anaerobic Adhesives—A Solution That Found a Problem" in *Living Case Histories of Industrial Innovation* (New York: Industrial Research Institute, 1981), pp. 24–27.

8. H. W. Coover, "Cyanoacrylate Adhesives—A Day of Serendipity, A Decade of Hard Work" in *Living Case Histories of Industrial Innovation* (New York: Industrial Research Institute, 1981), p. 28.

9. Peter C. Goldmark, "How the LP Record Was Developed—Or the Case of the Missing Fuzz" in *Living Case Histories of Industrial Innovation* (New York: Industrial Research Institute, 1981), p. 44.

10. Boorstin, op. cit., p. 86.

11. Edward B. Fiske, "Lessons of History Applied to the Present," *The New York Times,* 10 March 1981.

12. Robert Campbell, "Red," *Harvard Magazine,* September–October 1986, p. 111.

13. Stephen Jay Gould, *Ever Since Darwin* (New York: Norton, 1977), pp. 173–74.

14. Ibid., p. 177.

15. Devendra Sahal, *Patterns of Technological Innovation* (Reading, Mass.: Addison-Wesley, 1981), p. 66.

16. J. Patrick Wright, *On a Clear Day You Can See General Motors* (New York: Avon Books, 1979), p. 190.

17. Stephen Jay Gould, *Ever Since Darwin,* p. 208.

18. Peter F. Drucker, *Innovation and Entrepreneurship: Practices and Principles* (New York: Harper & Row, 1985), p. 192.

19. Alfred D. Chandler, Jr., *Strategy and Structure: Chapters in the History of the American Industrial Enterprise* (Cambridge, Mass.: MIT Press, 1962), p. 92.

20. Cited in Donald A. Schon, *The Reflective Practitioner: How Professionals Think in Action* (New York: Basic Books, 1983), p. 16.

21. George David Smith, *The Anatomy of a Business Strategy: Bell, Western Electric, and the Origins of the American Telephone Industry* (Baltimore: Johns Hopkins University Press, 1985), p. 79.

22. Cited in Robert Darnton, *The Great Cat Massacre and Other Episodes in French Cultural History* (New York: Basic Books, 1984), p. 192.

23. Ibid., p. 193.

24. Michael E. Parrish, *Securities Regulation and the New Deal* (New Haven: Yale University Press, 1970), p. 33.

25. Charles W. Parry, speech to The Newcomen Society (12 June 1985), Newcomen Publication No. 1249.

26. Earl Wiener, "Beyond the Sterile Cockpit," *Human Factors,* February 1985, p. 83.

27. David J. Rothman, *The Discovery of the Asylum: Social Order and Disorder in the New Republic* (Boston: Little, Brown, 1971), p. 108.

28. Elting E. Morison, in *Men, Machines, and Modern Times* (Cambridge, Mass.: MIT Press, 1966), pp. 17–18.

29. Richard N. Foster, *Innovation: The Attacker's Advantage* (New York: Summit, 1986).

30. See Richard F. Hirsh, "How Success Short-Circuits the Future," *Harvard Business Review,* March–April 1986.

31. Wayne G. Broehl, Jr., *John Deere's Company: A History of Deere & Company and Its Times* (Garden City, N.Y.: Doubleday, 1984), pp. 592–93.

32. Ibid., p. 593.

33. Margaret B. W. Graham, "Corporate Research and Development: The Latest Transformation," working paper, Boston University School of Management, 1985, pp. 14–15.

34. John P. McKelvey, "Science and Technology: The Driven and the Driver," *Technology Review,* January 1985, pp. 41–42.

35. Thomas M. McCraw, *Prophets of Regulation* (Cambridge, Mass.: Harvard University Press, 1984), p. 77.

36. Cited in Sidney H. Aronson, "Bell's Electrical Toy: What's the Use? The Sociology of Early Telephone Usage," in Ithiel de Sola Pool, ed., *The Social Impact of the Telephone* (Cambridge, Mass.: MIT Press, 1981), p. 23.

37. Daniel E. Whitney, "Real Robots Do Need Jigs," *Harvard Business Review*, May–June 1986.

38. Ernest R. May, *"Lessons" of the Past: The Use and Misuse of History in American Foreign Policy* (New York: Oxford University Press, 1973), p. ix.

39. Ibid., p. 177.

40. Leonard S. Reich, "Industrial Research and the Pursuit of Corporate Security: The Early Years of Bell Labs," *Business History Review*, Winter 1980, p. 528.

41. Peter F. Drucker, *Adventures of a Bystander* (New York: Harper & Row, 1978–79), p. 195.

42. Stephen Jay Gould, *The Panda's Thumb* (New York: Norton, 1982), pp. 28–29.

43. Paul Fussell, *The Great War and Modern Memory* (New York: Oxford University Press, 1975), p. 21.

44. F. Scott Fitzgerald, *Tender Is the Night* (New York: Scribner's, 1933), p. 57.

45. W. H. Auden, "Criticism in a Mass Society," *The Mint*, Vol. 2 (1948).

46. Eric Hobsbawm, "Introduction: Inventing Traditions," in Eric Hobsbawm and Terence Ranger, eds., *The Invention of Tradition* (Cambridge, England: Cambridge University Press, 1983), p. 1.

47. Ibid., p. 2.

48. Ibid., pp. 3–4.

49. Michael Polanyi, *The Tacit Dimension*, reprint ed. (Magnolia, Mass.: Peter Smith, 1983), pp. 4, 18.

50. Shoshana Zuboff, "Technologies that Informate: Implications for Human Resource Management in the Computerized Industrial Workplace," in Richard E. Walton and

Paul R. Lawrence, eds., *Human Resource Management: Trends and Challenges* (Cambridge, Mass.: Harvard Business School Press, 1985), pp. 111–12.

51. Hugh Trevor-Roper, "The Highland Tradition of Scotland," in *The Invention of Tradition*, p. 16.

52. Ibid., pp. 24–25.

53. George David Smith and John E. Wright, "Alcoa Goes Back to the Future," *Across the Board*, September 1986, p. 27.

54. Cited in David A. Hounshell, *From the American System to Mass Production, 1800–1932: The Development of Manufacturing Technology in the United States* (Baltimore: Johns Hopkins University Press, 1984), p. 217.

55. Elting Morison, op. cit., p. 42.

56. *Fortune*, 10 November 1986, p. 60.

57. Leonard W. Labaree et al., "Introduction," in Labaree et al., eds., *The Autobiography of Benjamin Franklin* (New Haven: Yale University Press, 1964), p. 31.

Index

DATE DUE

			Printed in USA

HIGHSMITH #45230